150+ *BEST*
PRACTICES FOR

B2B
MARKETING
SUCCESS:
NEXT-LEVEL STRATEGIES

150+ BEST PRACTICES FOR

B2B
MARKETING
SUCCESS:
NEXT-LEVEL STRATEGIES

ALEXANDER KESLER

Skyhorse Publishing

Skyhorse Publishing books may be purchased in bulk at special discounts for sales promotion, corporate gifts, fund-raising, or educational purposes. Special editions can also be created to specifications. For details, contact the Special Sales Department, Skyhorse Publishing, 307 West 36th Street, 11th Floor, New York, NY 10018 or info@skyhorsepublishing.com.

Skyhorse® and Skyhorse Publishing® are registered trademarks of Skyhorse Publishing, Inc.®, a Delaware corporation.

Visit our website at www.skyhorsepublishing.com.
Please follow our publisher Tony Lyons on Instagram @tonylyonsisuncertain

10 9 8 7 6 5 4 3 2 1

Library of Congress Cataloging-in-Publication Data is available on file.

Cover design by INFUSE

Print ISBN: 978-1-5107-8410-9
Ebook ISBN: 978-1-5107-8411-6

Printed in the United States of America

CONTENTS

INTRODUCTION

W elcome to *150+ Best Practices for B2B Marketing Success: Next-Level Strategies*, your comprehensive guide to navigating the intricate world of B2B marketing in today's dynamic landscape. Leveraging my experience in B2B marketing, I've witnessed the ebb and flow of trends, strategies, and challenges. The goal of this book is to encapsulate the wisdom I've received over those years into actionable insights and best practices that are both time-tested and well-adapted to the current market environment.

This book is a follow-up to *250+ Best Practices for B2B Marketing Success*. I've designed it with experienced marketers in mind, including seasoned veterans who are facing new challenges in an era of economic uncertainty and persistent budget cuts. In this edition, you'll find counsel on everything from leveraging intent-based marketing to measuring success and continuous optimization.

To make this guide as accessible as possible, **I've divided it into four parts** that loosely align with the order of the sales funnel from awareness to brand advocacy:

- **In part 1**, we'll lay the foundations for a robust B2B marketing strategy by exploring the nuances of defining ideal client profiles (ICPs) and leveraging data for precision targeting.
- **In part 2**, we'll focus on building out a comprehensive marketing strategy encompassing demand generation, account-based marketing, and content marketing, as well as channel and partner marketing.
- **In part 3**, we'll work our way through the buying journey to explore nurturing, conversion rate optimization, and revenue operations (RevOps) alignment.

- **In part 4,** we'll dive into best practices for evaluating success, driving continuous optimization, and staying one step ahead in the constantly evolving world of B2B marketing.

Finally, remember I'm not just the author, but also a practitioner who has faced many of the same challenges as you, and I'm dedicated to seeking solutions that will stand the test of time. If you ever wish to discuss any of the concepts in this book or need help with your B2B marketing strategy, feel free to get in touch with me at kesler@kesler.net.

I hope this book will serve as a valuable resource to help you grow a resilient business. Here's to mastering B2B marketing together!

– Alexander Kesler

PART ONE

UNDERSTANDING YOUR TARGET AUDIENCE

The world of B2B marketing is in a state of flux due to the ongoing effects of a global economic slowdown, budget cuts, ongoing layoffs, and constantly changing market conditions. Especially impacted are those in the technology and finance sectors, where many businesses have been forced to reevaluate and adapt their marketing strategies.

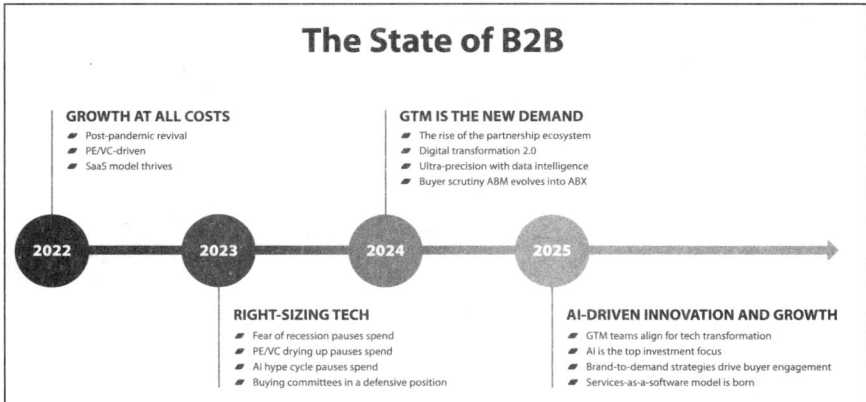

The State of B2B

GROWTH AT ALL COSTS
- Post-pandemic revival
- PE/VC-driven
- SaaS model thrives

GTM IS THE NEW DEMAND
- The rise of the partnership ecosystem
- Digital transformation 2.0
- Ultra-precision with data intelligence
- Buyer scrutiny ABM evolves into ABX

2022 — **2023** — **2024** — **2025**

RIGHT-SIZING TECH
- Fear of recession pauses spend
- PE/VC drying up pauses spend
- AI hype cycle pauses spend
- Buying committees in a defensive position

AI-DRIVEN INNOVATION AND GROWTH
- GTM teams align for tech transformation
- AI is the top investment focus
- Brand-to-demand strategies drive buyer engagement
- Services-as-a-software model is born

In the face of these ever-shifting circumstances, one fundamental truth persists: it is imperative to truly understand your target audience. While the buyer journey has evolved, so too have expectations, amplified by an increasingly competitive market landscape. It's not merely about the often-cited dwindling attention spans; it's the stark

1

decline in patience for vague, irrelevant, untargeted, and non-personalized marketing messages. That impatience is further exacerbated during times of economic uncertainty, leading to a growing trust deficit between businesses and their clients.

In-house research by INFUSE shows that about two thirds of marketers prioritize lead quality, while 60 percent are honing their full-funnel demand strategies. However, challenges persist. Nearly a third of marketers cite a lack of resources as their primary hurdle. Furthermore, the emphasis on personalization, though vital, is still far from becoming a universal practice, with only 40 percent of marketers actively working on improving it.

In part 1, we'll explore the foundational elements of a robust marketing strategy, including how to define your buyer personas and leverage quality data for precision targeting. Once you've taken those steps, you'll be ready to start a future-proof marketing strategy.

CHAPTER 1

DEFINING YOUR IDEAL CLIENT PROFILES

In the highly competitive world of B2B, casting a wide net often yields poor results. Success depends on precise targeting, and that begins with defining and understanding your ideal client. To make a real and lasting impact and ensure every message resonates, you need to know the needs, pain points, and desires of your target audience. Only then will you be able to build a strategy that aligns with genuine client needs.

#1 UNDERSTAND THE ROLE OF PERSONAS AND IDEAL CLIENT PROFILES

Relevance is key for succeeding in B2B marketing. This is all the more important now that the average number of touchpoints in the buyer's journey has increased to twenty-seven. Target audiences, buyer personas, and ideal client profiles (ICPs) serve as your guiding stars in ensuring you're sending the right message to the right people at the right time. Successful marketers typically use them in combination, but it's also important to understand how they differ.

The logical way to start is by defining your target audience. This encompasses the broader group of businesses you aim to reach, based on demographics and behavioral attributes. Marketers can leverage their target audiences to develop relevant content for the ever-evolving buying groups.

However, as buyers move through their buying journey, your messaging must become even more targeted. This requires a deeper understanding of the particular businesses and decision-makers you're working with. An ICP represents the business most likely to benefit from the purchase of your product or service, while your buyer personas are fictional representations of the decision-makers within those organizations that you'll be targeting.

By paying close attention to these factors when laying the foundations of your marketing strategy, you can ensure your messages resonate with buyers at each stage of their journey.

#2 GAIN A GRANULAR VIEW OF THE QUALITIES OF YOUR BUYER PERSONAS

To connect meaningfully with your target audience, surface-level insights won't suffice. The more granular your understanding of buyer personas, the better equipped your sales and marketing teams will be to build accurate strategies that align with buyer needs on an individual level and encourage decision-making in your favor.

Focusing on specific triggers, such as pain points and current business objectives, allows you to craft a targeted and relevant message. These triggers can then be leveraged to reveal the underlying motivations and challenges that drive your target audience's purchase decisions.

Approaches like social listening are also particularly effective. By monitoring and analyzing online conversations, you can garner a deeper understanding into the psychology of your audience. Moreover, these strategies can help you identify emerging trends, challenges, and topics of interest that can further inform your messaging. Equipped with this steady stream of real-time feedback, you can ensure your marketing strategies remain agile and responsive.

Surveys are another way to garner insight into your target audience and fine-tune your buyer personas accordingly. They offer a more structured approach to feedback by allowing you to present specific questions. When thoughtfully crafted and motivated, surveys can uncover hidden insights and reveal nuances that might not surface via more passive data-collection methods.

By combining these approaches and keeping a finger on the pulse of your target audience, you can ensure that every marketing initiative isn't only targeted, but is also deeply engaging and rigidly focused on building genuine connections.

#3 KNOW THE TYPES OF BUYER PERSONAS

A common oversight in marketing teams is to only leverage one type of buyer persona, usually the one most closely representing specific ICPs. The problem with this approach is that it leaves out occasional buyers and prospects who, while perhaps not an ideal match, may still benefit from your solutions or have an influence on purchase decisions.

There are three main types of buyer personas. Your primary one represents the key decision-makers in target accounts. They'll be the ones responsible for initiating, supporting, and even making the final purchase decision. Naturally, they should match your ICP.

A secondary buyer persona represents multiple individuals, so you'll ideally want a separate client profile for each one. Broadly speaking, these are people who might not have a direct and final say in purchase decisions, but are likely in a position to influence your primary buyer persona. For example, let's say you offer a SaaS (software as a service) solution for cybersecurity experts. While your primary buyer persona might be chief information security officers, your secondary buyer personas might encompass leaders in related departments like legal or compliance.

Finally, we have the often-overlooked negative buyer personas. Defining these can still be helpful, especially if you're having trouble with your targeting. As the term suggests, a negative buyer persona effectively defines the "red flags" that disqualify prospective buyers.

#4 STUDY YOUR AUDIENCE'S PREFERRED COMMUNICATION CHANNELS

There is no point in trying to reach buyers through channels they're unlikely to use, no matter how targeted your message. For example, if your target audience mostly frequents and engages with content on LinkedIn, that's where you'll want to focus the majority of your efforts, while ensuring that some budget is still dedicated to omnichannel outreach.

Given the plethora of social networks and other media channels available, it's vital to determine where your audience is most active. You also need to look beyond mainstream social media channels to include popular B2B databases like Crunchbase. Start by analyzing your current communications metrics, including engagement on social media and email response rates. Determine where conversion rates are currently highest, since this will provide valuable initial insight into where your audience is most active.

Also, remember that market preferences shift, especially in the constantly changing world of social media. Because of this, you shouldn't rely purely on historical data. By regularly surveying your audience with social listening tools, you can find where the important conversations related to your industry are happening.

Finally, consider the nature of each specific message when determining which channel to utilize. For example, a detailed product update might be better suited for a press release, blog post, or a guest post in a leading industry journal. By contrast, a quick, shorter announcement will likely gain more traction on LinkedIn or X, formerly known as Twitter.

#5 LAUNCH SURVEYS TO CAPTURE RELEVANT CLIENT DATA

Surveys offer a proven way to acquire relevant data. By developing online surveys and distributing them to your existing clients and prospects, you can learn more about their pain points, business goals, and preferences. Be sure to ask questions that help you understand how your audience finds and uses your solutions or those of competitors. This will further help you target your ideal client.

The power of surveys is their ability to provide actionable data. For example, they can reveal the specific trends and topics that resonate most with your target audience, thus guiding your content creation efforts. Moreover, surveys offer a great way to collect data in accordance with permission-based marketing, which is all the more important in the era of the General Data Protection Regulation (GDPR) and similar laws. This transparent approach not only adheres to regulatory standards but also builds trust and emphasizes your focus on client experience. After all, most people want their voices heard and are more than happy to share their opinions.

Other forms of user-generated content (UGC) that can provide helpful feedback are reviews, such as those on Trustpilot and G2 or collected via social listening platforms like Sprout Social. When used in combination with targeted surveys, you can collect valuable first- and third-party data to augment your targeting efforts.

#6 SEGMENT YOUR AUDIENCE BY INDIVIDUAL AND COMPANY ATTRIBUTES

Understanding your target audience goes beyond just knowing their job titles and industries. You need to take a holistic view of their firmographic, demographic, psychographic, and behavioral attributes to ensure your messaging is relevant.

For example, let's consider a SaaS company that sells an employee training and onboarding platform. Broadly speaking, the target audience will likely be HR leaders. However, there's a big difference in terms of needs, preferences, and pain points between HR leaders working in a company with upward of a thousand employees and those working for small startups with just a few dozen. A more detailed ICP might, for instance, be HR leaders in US companies with two-hundred-plus employees spread across a hybrid work environment and an annual revenue of $200 million or more.

But why stop at firmographics? You also need to remember that the recipient of your message isn't really a business, but an individual representing that business. That's why you also need to think about specific triggers, such as existing pain points, inefficiencies, and business goals. Understanding these influences helps greatly in crafting an effective engagement strategy that speaks to the individual, and not just to the business or department at large.

#7 IDENTIFY YOUR CLIENTS' KEY PAIN POINTS

Pain points are among the most common triggers of purchase decisions in the B2B world. They generally fall into four major categories: productivity, process, support, and finance. For example, productivity pain points may include inefficiencies in a competing product or service. A process pain point could be a stumbling point in a mission-critical business process, while a support pain point might be a lack of support during a particular stage of the buyer journey. Finally, a financial pain point might involve confusion around pricing structures or simply a fear of going over budget. Remember, any of these pain points could also be a factor in an existing client's use of your product, so it's important for client success and support teams to consider them too.

To identify client pain points, you can use surveys, focus groups, and interactive webinars. Sales, marketing, and client support teams, all of whom have firsthand knowledge of specific segments of the buyer journey, are also important sources of information on the various challenges that existing clients and buying groups face.

When identifying pain points for those closer to the top of the funnel, be sure to use social listening and competitive research. Not only will this help inform your messaging strategy, but it will also help you find an optimal market fit for your product or service.

#8   DEVISE DIFFERENT PERSONAS FOR EACH AUDIENCE SEGMENT

Many B2B products and services appeal to multiple industries and even different departments and stakeholders within each business. For example, every organization needs cybersecurity solutions, but precisely which solutions they need will depend on firmographic factors like sector and company size. To maximize your reach, you need to target every audience segment that matters most to you.

But, while it might sound counterintuitive, it's also possible to end up with too many buyer personas. This can dilute your messaging and become a burden on resources. It's important to start small, especially for startups and smaller companies. That said, most businesses should establish at least two distinct audience personas. Each of these should encompass industry-specific pain points, such as current market conditions and competitiveness, as well as regulatory requirements and industry standards.

By crafting these personas and gradually expanding your reach, you're iterating on a solid foundation for personalized marketing strategies. To that end, each persona becomes a guide, helping you tailor your content, product offerings, and communications so they resonate most with each audience.

#9   REVIEW AND UPDATE YOUR BUYER PERSONAS REGULARLY

The business landscape is ever-changing, especially if you're in the tech sector. Market shifts, evolving buyer behaviors, ever more advancing technology, and new pain points are inevitable. You must regularly review and edit your buyer personas to accommodate these updates. If you don't, it won't be long before your message becomes stale and outdated, losing its relevance in the process.

Consider, for example, some of the big changes we've seen in recent years. With the onset of the pandemic, remote work became the norm almost overnight. Since then, businesses have either remained fully remote, adopted a hybrid work model, or gone back to the old ways. Either scenario comes with its own set of challenges and opportunities, and it's essential that you stay up to date with their impact on your target audience.

While there's no hard-and-fast rule, it's generally best to review and update your buyer personas at least once per year. Moreover, you should always conduct a review whenever your company or the industry you serve undergoes a major change. For instance, if your company receives a major funding round or goes through M&A, it's a good time to review your buyer personas and broader marketing strategy. Similarly, new product or service launches are also ideal times to review and update your target personas.

CHAPTER 2

LEVERAGING DATA FOR PRECISION TARGETING

It's no secret that data is the lifeblood of any effective marketing strategy. However, with the immense amount of data at our fingertips, it's not just about collecting data, but also about using it effectively.

Precision targeting is the art of using data to pinpoint and engage your ideal clients with laser-focused accuracy. It's about predicting and understanding their needs to deliver a tailored message that makes a real and meaningful impact.

In chapter 2, we'll explore the collection and segmentation of firmographic, technographic, and behavioral data, as well as how to use it to gain a better understanding of buyer intent.

#10 REFINE YOUR FIRMOGRAPHIC SEGMENTATION WITH DATA ANALYTICS

One of the fundamental differences between B2C and B2B marketing is that the latter requires a deep understanding of your prospect's business and their unique challenges. That's where firmographic segmentation comes in, and it's arguably the most important tactic of all when identifying and qualifying your prospects.

This foundational step should typically come before you start delving into the psychology and demographics of the individuals you want to target within a given organization. Firmographics encompass industry, company size, annual revenue, location, sales cycle stages, company status, performance over time, and company structure. You can easily find firmographic data on popular B2B databases like Clutch.io and Crunchbase.

Knowledge of your prospect's industry is especially important, as it helps define their primary activities and gives you a starting point for understanding their key challenges. Annual revenue in combination with company size and status will help you determine a prospect's purchasing power. For example, a sole proprietor will have completely different needs from those of a large privately or publicly held company. Finally, understanding the company's structure will help you focus on the specific individuals to target within that company. In a smaller company or startup, for instance, one person may assume multiple roles.

#11 CATEGORIZE PROSPECTS BY GEOGRAPHIC SEGMENTATION WHERE RELEVANT

Be sure to segment your audience by geography before you start building out your individual client profiles. After all, the location of a prospect's company has a significant impact on purchasing power, local market conditions, industry standards, and regulations. For example, a small local business will have very different needs than a major international firm, even if they are in the same industry.

Geographic data should include country, region, city, and postal code (if applicable), all of which you should be able to find easily on the company's web page, social media, or a third-party B2B database. This will give you a starting point in researching key factors such as location-based industry and legal standards, cultural identity, and geopolitical landscape.

Depending on the industries you serve, geography also factors in changing seasons. For instance, two thirds of B2B companies experience a slump in sales during summer months. If you're targeting global companies in both hemispheres, you'll certainly want to take that into consideration.

#12 STUDY TARGET AUDIENCE DEMOGRAPHICS AS A STARTING POINT

Demographic segmentation is a foundational step to fine-tuning your audience personas. This involves collecting data from both existing and prospective clients based on variables such as age, annual income, education level, occupation, and job title. Each of these variables offers valuable insights into your audience's preferences and decision-making processes.

It's important to remember that some demographic attributes aren't as important as they once were, especially in the world of B2B. For example, factors like gender and marital status are largely irrelevant in most B2B sectors. Age, however, can still help inform the most appropriate messaging for specific target groups, especially when it comes to selecting marketing channels, voice, and style.

Annual income can also help qualify prospects in terms of buyer intent, while informing product teams about optimal pricing tiers and structures at the same time. However, since B2B purchases are usually made by businesses rather than individuals, this isn't as relevant as other metrics. For instance, knowledge of a prospect's education level and their professional experience is far more important. After all, there's no point in crafting highly technical content if your target audience isn't going to understand it.

Perhaps what is most important for B2B marketers is understanding a prospect's occupation and job title. For example, a CMO will likely have different needs, priorities, and pain points than those of a CFO or COO. Targeting the right job titles will help you evaluate people's decision-making power and processes. However, given the ever-evolving nature of B2B roles (especially in startups), it's important to take a nuanced view, as there may be inconsistencies regarding the specific responsibilities of team members in relation to their job titles.

#13 IDENTIFY KEY INFLUENCERS OF PURCHASE BEHAVIOR WITH PSYCHOGRAPHICS

While demographic segmentation offers surface-level insights into your audience, psychographic segmentation delves into the behavioral and emotional triggers that influence buying decisions. This approach is rooted in AIO variables (Activities, Interests, and Opinions), all of which are vital to understand when connecting with prospects on a cognitive level.

There's no better approach to precision targeting than getting a view into the minds of your potential clients. Psychographics help you better comprehend past behaviors and predict how future prospects with similar behavioral and emotional traits might act. This paves a path to predictive marketing strategies that enhance both lead acquisition and personalization. To that end, it's not just about knowing who your clients are (per demographics), but about understanding why they make the choices they make.

Psychographic attributes include personality traits, opinions, interests, hobbies, values, and lifestyle choices. You don't necessarily need to account for them all but be sure to include the ones that matter most in your industry in all your buyer personas.

As for collecting psychographic data, proven methods include conducting client interviews, analyzing social media, and tracking website analytics. Advanced solutions include sentiment analysis, which leverages modern technologies like natural language processing (NLP) to determine the emotional tone in large volumes of content like emails, client support chats, and social media comments.

#14 SEGMENT EXISTING CLIENTS BY USAGE RATE AND ACCOUNT STATUS

One of the most powerful ways to leverage data for precision targeting is by understanding how existing clients engage with your products and services. Also known as technographic segmentation, this strategy divides clients into groups based on how they use technology. Unsurprisingly, this is especially relevant if you're a SaaS company or any other tech vendor.

Start by breaking down your existing client base into heavy users, regular users, and occasional users:

- **Heavy users** are those who frequently engage with your products or services and have become dependent on them. They're also likely to be among your most satisfied clients.
- **Occasional users** only engage when a specific need arises, which might be due to the nature of your product. However, it might also point to difficulties they encounter when using your product.
- **Regular users** lie somewhere in between the two, but since they most likely account for the majority of your client base, they can serve as a baseline for setting your sales and marketing goals.

For service-based businesses, account status is another vital metric. For example, this may include active users, those who have paused or canceled their subscriptions, and those who are at risk of churning. Knowing the account status of your clients will help you tailor your marketing communication strategies, both for upselling and cross-selling, or when targeting prospective clients who might need more convincing.

#15 TRACK ONLINE BEHAVIOR TO UNDERSTAND BUYER INTENT

Intent data is behavioral information on a prospect's activity that indicates brand interest and their likelihood of buying your product or service. One of the most effective ways to track this is through your website analytics, which helps you determine what people are searching for to reach your website, as well as on your website.

Intent signals can come from multiple sources:

- **First-party intent data** originates from your own websites or other proprietary sources. In other words, it is data from prospects who have already interacted with your business in some way.
- **Second-party intent data** comes from sources like demand generation platforms and co-marketing campaigns.
- **Third-party intent data** typically includes cold prospects and originates from cookie and pixel systems, as well as industry research.

By overlaying multiple sources of first-, second-, and third-party data, you can gain a thorough understanding of what your target audience wants. However, make certain to label, tag, and manage your intent data in such a way as to preserve its quality and relevance. Also, be careful when collecting third-party intent data, since you can end up with misleading insights (as well as encounter privacy compliance issues). Once you've gathered the right data, you can use it to craft highly targeted marketing content.

#16 MEASURE BEHAVIORAL PATTERNS OVER EXTENDED PURCHASE PERIODS

If there's one constant in the world of marketing, it's change. Behavioral patterns change all the time, in line with economic realities, technical innovation, and other factors. That's why it's vital to measure behavioral patterns over time to better understand how people engage with your marketing content and products. In B2B, this is especially important because purchase periods tend to last months or multiple quarters, going through several stakeholders and approval rounds in the process.

Moreover, each of these stakeholders has a different set of purchase triggers, priorities, and processes. For example, a CFO might primarily be interested in pricing, while end users will likely be more concerned with productivity and efficiency.

Tracking prospects' interactions over time includes initial research, competitive research, and interactions with sales representatives. By understanding the unique behaviors of each target group, you can gain valuable insight into a prospect's intent and potential objections. This will also help you identify any barriers in the buyer journey, such as prospects running into issues during trial periods or finance teams questioning the viability of your pricing tiers.

#17 USE CREDIBLE FIRST-PARTY DATA SOURCES FOR EFFECTIVE LEAD AND ACCOUNT SCORING

The more first-party sources of intent data marketers use, the better. If you're only relying on one source of data to qualify intent, you may end up misunderstanding your prospects and segmenting them incorrectly.

You can retrieve quality data by measuring interactions and interests, such as internet searches, webinar attendance, and white paper downloads. For SaaS companies, in-app/platform usage metrics can also help track intent.

The key to success is to diversify your first-party data sources, as doing so will give you a big-picture view of what your prospects want. For instance, website analytics provide insights into how prospects reach specific web pages, how long they stay, and which actions they take. By contrast, webinar attendance and white paper downloads (when gated behind a lead capture page) indicate a deeper interest and a willingness to engage further.

Direct interactions, such as live chats, surveys, and client service inquiries, are important too, since they build on the aforementioned data sources to give you a more holistic view of your prospects. Remember, acquiring quality first-party data is even more important now that third-party cookies are gradually being phased out in accordance with global privacy legislation such as the GDPR and CCPA, as well as efforts by brands like Google and Apple.

#18 AUGMENT FIRST-PARTY DATA WITH SOCIAL PROOFING AND THIRD-PARTY INSIGHTS

First-party data might be the most valuable, but it takes time to collect, especially if you're in a relatively young business. That's why you need to augment it with second- and third-party insights and overlay these various sources of data.

For second-party data, the growing partner ecosystem is your most valuable resource. Examples include partner websites, co-hosted webinars and other events, affiliate marketing programs, co-branded content, and demand generation platforms. Also, look out for industry consortia and groups that share data among their members.

For third-party data, be sure to select trusted providers, such as INFUSE, Aberdeen, G2, and Cyance. These are among the most widely known providers. However, you'll need to check their compatibility with your existing tech stack, since the process involves handling massive amounts of data and integrating it with existing systems. You'll also need to cross-reference the data with other sources, so it's useful to have a data integration platform to enable more efficient processes.

#19 OPTIMIZE YOUR PRODUCT POSITIONING WITH NICHE MARKETING

Standing out in the vast B2B market has never been harder. A common mistake is trying to be everything to everyone. While that might get you website visits, at least for a time, it's not going to generate a qualified pipeline. Instead, you need niche marketing to appeal to those who are most likely to respond, as well as have the necessary purchasing power.

Product positioning is all about making your product or service as attractive as possible to your target audience. It's not a tangible goal with a specific finish line, but a steady brand-building process to ensure people perceive your brand positively. Clearly, that's not going to happen if your message ends up lost in all the white noise of social media and online content.

The data-driven segmentation strategies discussed earlier in this chapter can be powerful tools to inform your product positioning. This will also help you determine key details about competing products, thereby helping you establish a unique value proposition (UVP) and a distinct brand voice, tone, and style. Competitive research is vital, since you need to find a gap in the market where you can position your product in a viable way, without doing exactly the same thing as your competitors.

For example, while a deep analysis of psychographic data might not inform product research and development itself, it can help you tailor your messaging toward specific needs and pain points that your competitors are missing out on. In other words, it's not all about the product itself, but about communicating its unique value in a way that resonates with your target audience.

#20 DEPLOY ARTIFICIAL INTELLIGENCE TO SCALE DATA SEGMENTATION

Effective client segmentation relies on enormous amounts of data, so it's impractical for humans alone to analyze it. While your team will need to spend time extensively researching target audiences and building out their client profiles, machine learning and artificial intelligence can give you far deeper insight.

Some benefits of AI-augmented segmentation include the ability to identify hidden patterns in data and rapidly adapt client segments in a constantly changing market. Of course, the benefits of speed and scale shouldn't be understated either. A machine, after all, can scan through multiple gigabytes of data to detect patterns and trends in hours rather than weeks and months.

There are several methods for using machine learning and AI in client segmentation. For instance, clustering algorithms can segment clients into groups based on their behavioral, firmographic, and psychographic attributes. Decision trees can identify the key influences in prospect behavior during the buyer journey. Natural language processing (NLP) and neural networks offer even more powerful ways to identify recurring patterns in client behavior, as well as carry out sentiment analysis.

Popular SaaS solutions for AI-powered market segmentation include Bloomreach, Emarsys by SAP, and Klaviyo. Larger companies with data science teams and developers of their own may alternatively build proprietary solutions.

#21 PROMOTE DATA CLEANSING TO ELIMINATE LOW-QUALITY DATA

An abundance of data isn't always a good thing. The reality is that a lot of data is poor quality, outdated, or irrelevant. Without regular data cleansing and matching, you can end up with a severely polluted database.

Proven ways to combat data quality issues include ridding your databases of duplicate entries, incomplete records, and mismatched metadata. Once again, this is something that you can really only do with the help of AI and machine learning, simply due to the massive scale of today's datasets making manual analysis and optimization impossible.

Schedule regular audits to ensure your data remains current and accurate. Exactly how often you do this depends on factors like database size and growth, but it should typically tie in with the regular reviews of your buyer personas as mentioned in chapter 1, item 9.

Naturally, prevention is the best cure, so it's also a good idea to implement measures that help you maintain data quality whenever new data is added into the system. For example, you can standardize formats and use data validation tools to verify things like email addresses or social media profiles. Finally, be sure to establish an effective feedback mechanism with your sales and client support teams and train them on the importance of data quality to prevent issues from arising further down the line.

#22 GO BEYOND MQLs WITH BUYER-CENTRIC QUALIFICATION MODELS

B2B buyers have increasingly adopted an independent, defensive stance, relying on self-conducted research and often connecting with sales reps only after having completed 70–80 percent of their buyer's journey.

During this research stage, prospects often fill out lead capture forms in their search for content to support their decision-making process. This behavior, irrespective of its intent or the prospect's readiness to engage, contributes to their lead score, resulting in prospects being forwarded to sales teams for follow-up ahead of time.

Thus, the arbitrary relation between lead score and activity results in MQL-based qualification models often mistaking engagement for purchase intent. This also contributes to teams failing to identify truly in-market buyers and accounts and mistiming their sales outreach, a frustrating process for both sides.

Combined with the emphasis on marketing to support sales goals, this has led to 47 percent of B2B demand marketers affirming that generating sales-ready leads represents one of their biggest challenges, according to INFUSE's Voice of the Marketer research. Buyer-centric qualification models are therefore key to understanding the true behavior of today's B2B buyers, contributing to an advantageous positioning.

These models leverage a combination of technographic data, research intent signals, and ICPs/buyer personas, in addition to more traditional criteria such as pain points and budgetary restrictions. This strategy is also supported by demand intelligence collected from existing high-value clients, informing optimizations. Buyer-centric models must be developed with the collaboration of all teams to ensure that they leverage the most relevant and actionable information. Then, insights from this method can in turn be reshared across the organization to bolster future efforts.

#23   ITERATE AND IMPROVE ON YOUR DATA COLLECTION AND ANALYSIS PROCESSES

As buyer behavior and preferences change and evolve over time, so must your qualification criteria in order to ensure the actionability and relevance of the data insights you collect. Therefore, reevaluating the efficiency of your data collection and analysis processes is essential to guarantee that your campaigns leverage data to its full potential.

Each campaign can also offer valuable insights into the validity and gaps in your qualification criteria, as well as data analysis processes. Criteria that are successfully leveraged by your teams to achieve increased performance and ROI should be maintained and improved upon as much as possible. On the other hand, data points that do not lead to improvements must be phased out to declutter databases and minimize data collection.

Additionally, feedback from other teams, especially those in direct contact with clients, can help optimize future iterations. For example, a commonly unknown factor is the budget at the disposal of each buying group at target accounts, creating difficulties for sales teams looking to create personalized outreach. Therefore, crafting touchpoints in the buyer journey dedicated to identifying this information can be incredibly informative for guiding sales strategies and promoting a better buying experience. Companies are often reluctant to discuss their budgets openly, so questions that can provide you with a ballpark estimate, such as company size, as well as the number of clients and team members who will benefit from your solution, are good substitutes. However, it is crucial to ensure your data processing complies with present and forthcoming privacy regulations as they arise.

#24 IMPLEMENT A SINGLE SOURCE OF TRUTH FOR CLIENT DATA ACROSS ALL DEPARTMENTS

The value of interdepartmental alignment and the hindrances caused by data silos have long been discussed as a universal issue in business. Ensuring that prospect data and insights are made available to all teams becomes even more crucial for delivering the seamless, personalized experiences today's buyers have come to expect.

Organization-wide and cross-departmental meetings are a traditional approach to sharing data insights across teams, helping everyone work toward the same goal. However, compiling all this data into a single system, offering a unified, real-time analytics dashboard to all teams, provides visibility vital for performance analysis and optimization.

This is especially prudent as companies race to activate AI to bolster sales and marketing efforts. Keeping all data united on a single source of truth streamlines and empowers their implementation, enabling truly transformative data-driven decision-making.

#25 MAINTAIN FULL COMPLIANCE WITH INTERNATIONAL PRIVACY REGULATIONS

As the general public develops awareness regarding the value of personal data and the crucial importance of its protection, government bodies across the world have strived to define laws and regulations concerning the collection, storage, and use of customer data. Failing to comply with these policies can not only incur significant financial losses but also risk damage to a company's reputation and brand equity.

Today's defensive buyers value word-of-mouth referrals and online reviews as unbiased sources of information. For this reason, the fallout from such reputational damage can be even more detrimental to company finances than the fines themselves. Additionally, as high-value prospects and PE/VC investors also become increasingly concerned with data protection, a lack of well-established processes to ensure compliance will surely lead to lost opportunities.

Reducing data collection to the minimum possible, implementing strict internal privacy guidelines, ensuring user consent, and anonymizing data are some key measures to avert these risks. Accessible, transparent, and easy-to-understand policies detailing your company's data usage can also help build trust. Be sure to stay ahead of any future legislation in development, paving the way for both effortless compliance and expansion to other markets, often subject to different laws and regulations.

Another crucial measure is to ensure your current and potential business partners follow similar measures to avoid collateral damage from possible malpractice.

Finally, remember that it is your responsibility to protect your data from malicious access. Therefore, industry-leading cybersecurity measures, from sophisticated encryption algorithms to secure data transfer protocols, also become indispensable for safely managing your data.

#26 FOCUS ON COLLECTING FIRST-PARTY DATA RATHER THAN RELYING ON EXTERNAL VENDORS

In early 2020, Google announced plans to phase out cookie support on its Chrome browser, sending shock waves through the marketing industry, accustomed to relying on third-party data to fuel strategies. Although the company has since substituted this measure for the implementation of more user-friendly privacy controls, the available pool of third-party, cookie-based data is still foreseen to be significantly reduced.

Standard privacy regulations usually do not prohibit the usage of cookies, instead requiring clear user consent before placement. Such consent, however, can be considerably more difficult to ascertain in the case of third-party data providers. In addition, the reputational damage of potential legal sanctions to data vendors may spread to their clients as well, increasing risk.

Hence, many companies have begun to prepare a solid first-party database to inform their marketing strategies. In addition to future-proofing against any potential changes to third-party cookie systems, first-party data collection is highly customizable, earning deeper, more actionable insights into user behavior and preferences. It also grants users more control over their data and its utilization, fostering trust and enabling greater personalization. While requiring a notable investment of time and resources, first-party data ultimately achieves higher revenue and contributes to reduced acquisition costs.

Although third-party data providers can still offer actionable information, preparing a first-party database is crucial to ensure long-term performance, as data from each campaign feeds back into optimizations. This way, companies can deliver increasingly valuable experiences driven by custom-tailored, highly relevant content; this ultimately leads to increased ROI.

PART TWO

CRAFTING YOUR MARKETING STRATEGY

To stay relevant in an increasingly unpredictable market, businesses must be proactive. This involves targeting and adapting marketing investments based on how different audience personas behave at different stages of the funnel. For example, while C-suite members are usually responsible for purchase decisions, they will likely rely on assistants and other staff to research and collate opinions. As such, these personas play an important role higher up the funnel, and it's vital to build a marketing strategy that considers that.

Proprietary research by INFUSE found that C-suite members engage with a brand under 2 percent of the time. Moreover, according to the LinkedIn B2B Institute, only 5 percent of an organization's total addressable market (TAM) has the intent to buy. That's why marketers need to build a demand generation engine that prioritizes full-funnel tactics.

In part 1, we explored the foundational steps of defining your audience personas. Next comes the strategy. In part 2, we'll look at four proven B2B marketing strategies: demand generation, account-based marketing, and content marketing, as well as channel and partner marketing.

Once you've established a full-funnel marketing system incorporating these crucial elements, you'll be able to identify and nurture qualified leads and maximize your marketing ROI.

CHAPTER 3
BUILDING A DEMAND GENERATION STRATEGY

$\mathbf{D}$emand generation is, as the name suggests, a set of sales and marketing activities designed to increase the demand for your products and services.

The process broadly spans four stages, beginning with spreading awareness of your product. Next is to generate interest with the help of value-adding content and a concise, benefit-driven marketing message. After that comes product positioning and driving conversions, both strategies that revolve around showcasing your unique value proposition (UVP) and competitive differentiators. Finally, you have retention and expansion, which center on nurturing existing clients and turning them into brand advocates.

In this chapter, we'll explore what goes into creating a demand generation strategy spanning the entire sales funnel.

#27 DEVELOP A NORTH STAR TO GUIDE YOUR ORGANIZATION'S ACTIVITIES

Developing cohesive, long-term marketing plans that demonstrate quantifiable value is an ongoing challenge. However, aligning strategies with a well-established core objective, tied to the company's overarching goals, can streamline and inform planning. Such is the value of working under a North Star: a revenue-attributable, long-term vision for the organization as a whole.

The purpose of a North Star is to anchor day-to-day activities to aspirational goals, guiding interdepartmental efforts toward a common purpose. It should be built in collaboration with different teams to ensure achievability and appropriate scope to ensure that it serves as a feasible and motivational goal for the organization.

Rallying around a North Star helps teams develop and identify tasks that contribute to common goals, guiding strategic thinking and decision-making. North Star objectives also inform tracking strategies, highlighting the key indicators that feed directly into your core vision. The development of a North Star can also inform your messaging, as this process includes identifying core competitive positioning, and anchoring strategies around your unique value proposition (UVP).

Much like other strategic initiatives, your North Star must also undergo auditing and reviewing, ensuring it accurately reflects the company's needs/focus as they evolve.

#28 UNDERSTAND THE FULL SALES FUNNEL

Demand generation is a comprehensive approach that goes beyond the top of the sales funnel (TOFU). It's not just about attracting leads but identifying entire buying groups, nurturing them throughout their buying journey and even beyond the sale to the point of brand advocacy. A successful demand generation strategy should focus on removing friction from the buyer journey to ensure a seamless and consistent client experience.

To create compelling content, you need to understand how your buyer personas engage with your business at each stage of the funnel. At the TOFU stage, the main goal is to generate interest. Content is typically educational, aimed at a relatively large audience and addressing more general pain points. It's also the time to start establishing your brand as an industry authority.

At the middle of the sales funnel (MOFU) stage, your message should become more targeted, addressing specific challenges and aligning them with the solutions your products or services offer. This stage is all about building trust and reducing uncertainty. Content at this stage might include webinars, case studies, white papers, and product demonstrations.

Finally, we have the bottom of the sales funnel (BOFU), where prospective buyers are primed for conversion. At this point, you have qualified leads who are already considering investing in your product or service. As such, content should be geared toward closing the deal, so you'll be looking at tactics like consultations, free trials, and in-depth product demonstrations.

#29 LEVERAGE BRAND-TO-DEMAND FRAMEWORKS

Focusing marketing on brand goals, such as awareness or authority, is by no means a novel concept. However, the period of economic uncertainty following the COVID pandemic pressured marketers to emphasize short-term results, concentrating efforts on tactics such as the generation of sales-ready leads to ensure a steady flow of revenue. Conversely, this overt focus on short-term goals hindered longer-term marketing initiatives based on fostering brand awareness and client relationships, especially given the difficulty of attributing revenue to these tactics.

However, as buyer behavior evolves, long-term brand plays are becoming once again essential to ensure future growth. Indeed, buyers have become more independent, further complexifying buyer journeys. On average, today's buyers contact vendors 70–80 percent of the way through their buying journey. As a result, prospects now spend most of their journeys interacting with brands on their own schedule, guided by their needs and interests, which makes investing in a compelling brand experience indispensable for successful demand generation. Furthermore, the widely known 95–5 rule—stating that, at any given time, only 5 percent of a brand's potential buyers are looking to purchase—contributes to the importance of long-term brand building.

Hence the renewed focus on brand-to-demand marketing, a buyer-centric model integrating brand awareness into demand generation efforts. Not only does this approach lay the foundation for demand among the 95 percent of your audience not currently in-market, it also contributes to promoting the seamless buying experience increasingly expected by today's buyers.

Centered on the principle that brand efforts do not detract from the success of demand strategies and vice versa, brand-to-demand marketing promotes a homogeneous experience from discovery to purchase, as both brand and demand are intrinsically linked.

#30 ADOPT BUYER-CENTRIC STRATEGIES

Buying groups now feature more members from younger generations (millennials and Gen Z) in decision-making roles. As a result, these groups as a whole have become more tech-savvy, with greater command of their purchase processes than ever. Demanding greater value and in-depth expertise from vendors, buyers have come to expect more personalized experiences, in which products and services are adapted to their unique needs.

Marketers must therefore bridge the gap between expectations and facilitate the buying process. For the independent buyer, fostering brand awareness and building trust are essential to driving sales interactions.

Buyers commonly approach sales with the requirements for their purchase already fully determined. This places greater emphasis on the role of strategies that contribute to brand value, such as content and nurturing efforts. To support a buyer-centric experience, these strategies must enable self-paced learning and de-risk decision-making, simplifying buying processes.

Sales teams must also contribute to this by adopting a supportive approach, offering on-demand consultation to personalize experiences, rather than pushing for a sale at all costs.

#31 DEFINE YOUR UNIQUE VALUE PROPOSITION

Your unique value proposition (UVP) is the cornerstone of your demand generation strategy. It's what sets you apart from the competition and helps you identify the right market fit for your product. It should succinctly communicate the primary benefit of using your product or service. Indeed, a UVP should be easily understood within seconds of a prospect learning about your business. If what you can do for your clients is not instantly clear from your home page and social media profiles, then people won't stick around.

The best way to define a UVP is to list the features and benefits your product offers and align them with the needs and pain points of your ideal client profiles. Distill that information down into a single sentence that will serve as the basis for your marketing communications.

Your UVP should answer the *who*, *what*, and *why*. American entrepreneur Steve Blank offers one of the simplest approaches to crafting a UVP: "We help X do Y by doing Z." For example, a value proposition for a freelance-based B2B translation company might be: "We help companies engage their global clients' emotions by delivering resonant messaging in their native languages."

You'll likely want more than one UVP, especially if you target multiple industries or have more than one product. Ideally, you should have one UVP per ideal client profile.

#32 ESTABLISH A CONSOLIDATED BRAND VOICE

B2B marketing content is often lamented for being dry and boring, but it doesn't have to be. Every successful brand has a personality, a consistent expression spanning across both written and visual content. A strong brand voice comes with psychological and experiential associations that tell the story of who your company is.

Defining and consolidating your brand voice is an internal process to be shared across every department, especially those that are client-facing, such as sales, marketing, and client success. It should encompass your mission, vision, values, and of course, your UVP.

Your brand mission is your purpose, answering the question of why you're in business. It's not just a mission statement, but something that's lasting and meaningful and conveys your message to both employees and clients.

Your brand vision is your perspective. It's a statement detailing where your business aspires to be in the future. A brand vision statement typically focuses more on employees, as well as stakeholders and investors (if relevant).

Brand values refer to the promises you make to your employees, clients, and the broader community around your business. They're a fundamental part of corporate social responsibility (CSR) and environmental, social, and governance (ESG) initiatives, but they'll also come to play an important role in your messaging.

Wrapping it all up under a consolidated brand voice requires choosing tone, colors, and other design elements that you'll use across your marketing collateral. This should broadly align with your industry, the expectations of your target audience, the knowledge levels of your personas, and your core values.

#33 CREATE STYLE GUIDELINES FOR ALL MARKETING COMMUNICATIONS

When creating a B2B marketing strategy spanning multiple channels and involving multiple departments, it's easy to lose sight of the consolidated brand voice mentioned earlier. This should span the visual design and language and tone of all your marketing collateral, from display ads to blog posts to white papers and everything in between. Failing to establish the necessary standards and guidelines will lead to inconsistency and confusion, which can imply a lack of collective vision from your company.

A gold standard for creating style guidelines is to publish a brand book. These documents are meant to inspire and guide your team on everything from your tone of voice to your logos, color palettes, and iconography. In many ways, a brand book is a piece of marketing collateral itself, albeit one intended for your internal teams and any outsourced teams or freelancers you work with.

Brand books and style guides can seem very business-minded and are often known for being dull and overly formal, especially in the B2B world. But that doesn't have to be the case. A great brand book isn't just an uninspiring collection of rules, but an engaging set of guidelines accentuated by a healthy dose of personality. In demand generation marketing, that consistent personality carries over to reinforce credibility and foster stronger relationships with your audience.

#34 DEVELOP SEAMLESS USER AND CLIENT EXPERIENCES

Building a robust demand generation engine focuses on both the product or service you offer and how you deliver it. Positive digital experiences foster loyalty, drive conversions, and help set you apart from your competitors. If you don't offer seamless user and client experiences, even the most outstanding products will end up unnoticed and underappreciated.

User experience (UX) focuses on the user's interaction with your product or platform, thus it typically falls under the purview of a dedicated UX team. Client experience, by contrast, refers to the entire journey a client undertakes with a company, from their initial touchpoint to their final interaction, along with all the steps in between.

As the lines between B2C and B2B user experience blur, businesses must prioritize ease of use and strive to remove sources of friction that result in buyers and buying groups dropping out of consideration. For example, when it comes to UX, digital platforms should typically be mobile responsive, as that's how many B2B decision-makers now consume content.

As for client experience, common barriers include confusion over pricing structures, a lack of timely client support, and a lack of targeted content to assuage decision-makers' concerns. Given the length and complexity of the typical B2B buyer journey, developing a quality client experience is vital for generating demand and retaining existing clients.

#35 PROMOTE CONTENT WITH PAID ADVERTISING

Advertising is where demand generation began. Even in the age of organic outreach, advertising is still one of the most reliable ways to generate demand, especially when you need to drive awareness at scale and achieve results quickly. Thus, it can be particularly effective when launching a new product or entering a new market. However, as it requires paying for advertising space, targeting the right people through the right channels is crucial for maximizing ROI.

Pay-per-click (PPC) advertising is one of the most recognized forms of advertising. Platforms like Google Ads allow businesses to promote text and image ads targeting specific keywords across one of the world's biggest ad networks. The strength of PPC advertising is that you only have to pay when someone engages with your ad, making it easier to measure and optimize your ROI.

Targeted display ads are another popular tactic. They're more dynamic and flexible than PPC ads, since you can include interactive elements like search and booking functions. These ads typically use machine-learning algorithms to automatically select optimal placements across publisher networks, such as the Google Display Network. You can also set daily advertising criteria and budgets with most providers.

Though traditionally more closely associated with B2C markets, influencer marketing can also be effective in B2B. It allows you to tap into the large following of thought leaders and trusted individuals in your industry. However, because any brand's reputation hinges on that of their advertising partners, it's essential to choose influencers whose behavior aligns with your brand values and industry.

#36 DETERMINE WHERE TO GATE CONTENT BEHIND A LEAD CAPTURE PAGE

Gated content refers to any content that requires a visitor to complete a form on a lead capture page to gain access to it. Content gating can be a powerful demand generation method, but you should only use it for high-value assets, such as eBooks and white papers. In other words, the content needs to be compelling enough for your audience to willingly exchange their contact details for access.

It's not always an easy balance to get right, so you'll want to use content gating sparingly and strategically, ideally around the MOFU stage of the buyer journey. Avoid using it with TOFU content, such as blog posts, as you may risk alienating prospective buyers who are still in the first stages of engaging with your business. On the other hand, if you don't gate at all, especially at the MOFU or BOFU stages, you risk missing out on valuable lead capture information and intent signals.

Gated landing pages should be optimized for conversions. That means having a clear, concise form that only asks for the absolute essentials: usually a name, job title, company name, and email. The accompanying landing page content should be similarly concise, listing the main highlights of the gated content in a compelling, value-driven way. Remember, the goal is to make the exchange of information feel worthwhile, so make sure it aligns with their needs, interests, and pain points.

#37 FOCUS ON COMMUNITY BUILDING AND MARKETING

Fostering a sense of community is a game changer in B2B marketing. It's not about amassing a following, but about cultivating genuine relationships, building trust, and creating a space in which your target audience feels valued and heard. By building and nurturing your community, you're promoting not only your products or services but also your brand and its mission and values. Moreover, it encourages an exchange of knowledge that bolsters brand loyalty and provides valuable feedback.

Most popular brands have communities, even if they don't formally have ownership of them. Community marketing takes things a step further by allowing you to leverage the power of community to drive awareness, engagement, and conversions. Branded communities typically reside on client forums, dedicated social media groups, or even proprietary mobile apps with social elements built in.

The great thing about having your own community is that you have control over it. You get to set the rules and standards and steer the conversation. That said, it's vital to engage regularly, showcase valuable user-generated content (UGC), and work closely with the most influential members of your community. Ideally, you'll want to appoint a community head and a team of moderators. After all, ending up with a dead community on your website is far worse than having no community at all.

#38 IMPLEMENT AN EFFECTIVE ATTRIBUTION MODEL

An attribution model helps you determine which department is responsible for generating demand, converting to pipeline, and contributing to revenue. It can inform important decisions regarding budgeting and resource distribution. By pinpointing the precise moment a prospective buyer decides to make a purchase or exchange their contact details, you can easily understand which parts of your marketing campaign are working and which ones need improvement. Here are some commonly used attribution models for B2B demand generation:

- **First-touch attribution:** This credits the first touchpoint a prospect interacts with before converting. This approach puts the emphasis on TOFU activities and includes elements like ad clicks, email open rates, or website clicks in search results.
- **Last-touch attribution:** This credits the last touchpoint in the buyer journey. It highlights the final interactions that lead to a conversion, making it especially important in omnichannel marketing programs.
- **Linear attribution:** This approach distributes credit equally across all touchpoints that a prospect interacts with. By recognizing the value of each interaction, it's particularly relevant in B2B given the typically longer and more complex sales cycles.
- **Full-path attribution:** This model captures the entire client journey from their first interaction to the closed deal and, in some cases, even post-sale interactions. Since it considers all stages of the buying process, it's especially valuable in B2B.
- **Algorithmic attribution:** This newer strategy uses machine learning to assign credit based on the actual impact a given touchpoint has on conversions. This model is very dynamic and can adjust to data trends.
- **Account-level attribution:** This method considers all the touchpoints across individuals within the same company, making it especially relevant for scenarios where there are multiple stakeholders involved in the purchase decision.

The best attribution model suits the complexity of your buyer journey and the number of people involved in the purchase decision. However, B2B marketers usually favor the more involved attribution models, such as full-path, algorithmic, and account-level attribution.

#39 DEFINE THE GOALS OF YOUR DEMAND GENERATION CONTENT STRATEGY

To truly harness the power of demand generation marketing, it's vital to have a clear vision of the desired results of each tactic you use. For example, if you're publishing a sales enablement document highlighting your UVP, its primary objective might be to distinguish your offers from those of competitors.

Crafting impactful marketing collateral requires aligning your content with brand guidelines and goals. For instance, content that aligns with your brand mission and messaging could include snackable assets that focus on core values and can be promoted on social media sites or using targeted display ads. By contrast, strategies focused on building loyalty and competitive positioning might include campaigns to incentivize clients to leave reviews or events with thought leaders promoting solutions to major market challenges.

Every piece of content you publish should have a measurable goal to help you understand what's working and what isn't. Blog posts might serve primarily to increase search traffic, case studies and white papers to build trust and authority, and webinars to engage prospects on a more personal level. Whatever you're doing to further your demand generation strategy, it should have a distinct purpose that aligns with your broader business goals and priorities.

#40 MAP OUT YOUR CONTENT WITH A PUBLISHING CALENDAR

Once you've established your goals and style guide, it's time to map out your content. After all, any marketing strategy is only as effective as the planning that goes into its execution. A content calendar helps you maintain a consistent publishing schedule, keep track of goals and deadlines, and ensure your content reaches the right audience at the right time.

In most cases, a simple spreadsheet will suffice, but once your marketing strategy expands, it might be more effective to use a project management tool. That way, you can easily visualize which assets you've created and which ones are in your content pipeline. To make planning even more effective, be sure to align content with overarching business goals and the specific stages of the buyer journey that they're most relevant to.

Campaign-focused organization is also beneficial, especially as you scale up your demand generation strategy. This involves clustering related topics, along with the audience personas they're most relevant to, allowing you to create marketing campaigns in which longer pieces of content are supported by shorter, related assets.

For example, a white paper may serve as the central piece in a given campaign, but, to maximize its effectiveness, you'll need supporting content like landing pages, blog posts, and social media posts. Remember, as your strategy evolves, so too should your publishing calendar, so that it always remains in line with your broader marketing efforts and marketing channel strategies.

#41 BOOST EFFICIENCY WITH SOCIAL LISTENING

Social listening tools allow you to track brand mentions and branded keywords. You can set up alerts whenever they're published on social media. Social listening is especially powerful in helping you understand how target audiences talk about your brand on platforms that aren't tracked by analytics. It also helps you monitor and analyze conversations at a scale that would otherwise be impossible. After all, conversations about brands and products happen around the clock across numerous online platforms.

When combined with natural language processing (NLP) and sentiment analysis, social listening also helps you monitor broader attitudes toward your brand. Moreover, you can use it to monitor trends in your industry. This, in turn, informs your content and adds relevance to your demand generation campaigns. By keeping an ear to the ground, you can also identify who your brand advocates and industry influencers are.

Conversely, social listening lets you quickly identify dissatisfied clients and misinformation, giving you the opportunity to take corrective action before they severely damage your brand image.

Popular social listening tools include Sprout Social, Hootsuite, Zoho Social, and Reputation. These all-in-one social media management platforms help you keep track of what people are saying about your brand on social media and make it easier to manage your company's reputation.

#42 PROMOTE YOUR CONTENT THROUGH SOCIAL MEDIA AND EMAIL

Successful demand generation requires an integrated marketing plan that involves creating and promoting content in the right places at the right times. Without careful distribution and timing, your content is much less likely to succeed, no matter how good it is. After all, you can't expect content to promote itself, which is why you should make social media, email, and other distribution methods integral to the process.

As with content creation itself, promotion and distribution should be informed by an in-depth knowledge of target audiences, their preferred channels, and the stage of the purchase funnel they're at. An omnichannel strategy, backed up with a clear attribution model as we talked about earlier, will minimize the risk of wasted time and budgets. There are three main ways to distribute content:

- **Owned content distribution** involves publishing content on channels you control, such as your website or social media profile pages.
- **Earned content distribution** refers to publishing content on third-party channels, such as guest blog posts and review sites.

- **Paid content distribution** includes PPC advertising, programmatic display advertising, and influencer or affiliate marketing.

We'll explore these various channels and how to work with them in greater depth in chapter 6.

#43 KEEP TRACK OF SHORT-TERM PERFORMANCE INDICATORS, BUT PRIORITIZE LONG-TERM RESULTS

By nature, demand generation is a long-term strategy, typically building up across the entirety of a buying cycle, which lasts an average of eleven to twelve months. Given the length and breadth of demand generation strategies throughout buying journeys, results must be quantified by measuring both short- and long-term outcomes across campaigns, helping stakeholders track progress and informing on-flight optimizations.

A key strategy is to identify achievable, short-term goals that pave the way for the campaign's long-term vision. KPIs such as click-through rates, user engagement, and followership, for example, relate directly to demand performance and support revenue generation, since prospects that regularly interact with your content and benefit from its value are more likely to think of your company when approaching bottom-of-funnel stages. Conversely, conversion rates and booked meetings illustrate the more immediate ROI of demand generation strategies, indicating how prospects that are already familiar with your brand and its offerings navigate the final stages of their buying process.

#44   BOLSTER THE LONG-TERM NATURE OF DEMAND GENERATION WITH SHORT-TERM PLAYS

Focusing on the long-term outcomes of demand generation marketing, however, does not mean forgetting short-term strategies. On the contrary, these strategies can work in tandem with a demand framework to drive holistic, full-funnel results that none of them would achieve separately.

Display ads, PPC, search ads, SEO/GEO/AEO, and other performance marketing tactics are highly valuable to attract prospective buyers into your nurturing cadences, by boosting the visibility of tactical assets such as free tools and white papers. This, in turn, contributes to cementing your reputation as a trustworthy solution provider in the industry.

After all, the goal of demand strategies is to accompany prospective buyers throughout their entire buyer's journey by continuously providing them with value. In this way, demand strategies, when carefully orchestrated according to the evolving buyer needs across buying stages, consolidate brand authority, foster trust, and lay the foundations for conversions.

CHAPTER 4
MASTERING ACCOUNT-BASED MARKETING

Account-based marketing is a targeted growth strategy that brings sales and marketing teams together to create personalized buying experiences. This method centers on identifying high-value companies, known as accounts, which are most likely to benefit from specific solutions. To that end, ABM zeroes in on the needs, challenges, and opportunities of target accounts, effectively treating each one as a unique market.

ABM follows the idea that, in B2B marketing, purchase decisions are often made by a group of stakeholders within a company, rather than an individual. This group, often referred to as the "buying committee" or "buying group" may include members from various departments, such as IT, finance, operations, and executive leadership.

In the typical progression of B2B marketing, ABM often follows demand generation by focusing on the highest-value buyers. However, the two may also run concurrently, and the lines can blur. In this chapter, we'll focus on the role of hyper-personalization and building relationships with your most promising buyers and buying groups.

#45 ALIGN YOUR STAKEHOLDERS ACROSS BUSINESS FUNCTIONS

Successful ABM necessitates alignment between sales and marketing teams to create a cohesive buyer's journey. This ensures that everyone is equipped with the information necessary to engage accounts at the right time and through the right channels. The goal is to enable a seamless, personalized experience that moves prospects through their buying journey and eliminates sources of friction along the way.

Without organization-wide structure and alignment, demonstrating the impact of campaigns at different stages of the sales pipeline is challenging. This is a common problem in businesses that try to silo ABM in a single department or stakeholder. Instead, to achieve the desired results, you need to form a multidisciplinary team with stakeholders across business functions.

Account managers play a central role in ABM, since they're responsible for communicating with both new and existing clients and coordinating with departments to create and implement targeted campaigns. They'll be on the front lines of the entire process. They're deeply involved in client success and bridging the gaps between sales and marketing. A typical ABM team structure also brings together content managers and creators, marketing operations leaders, field marketers, and sales development representatives (SDRs).

#46 CONNECT WITH BUYING GROUPS ON SOCIAL MEDIA

Many marketers still commonly assume B2B marketing is all about one-to-one interactions. However, according to Gartner, the average buying group has between fourteen and twenty-three people. The size of buying groups also tends to grow if the pricing is high, as well as the number of people and departments that will be using the product.

Targeting the entire buying group requires more work than focusing only on primary audience personas, but it's far more effective in cases that involve multiple stakeholders and departments in purchase decisions. It allows you to discover and target secondary personas too, as well as influencers and potential referral opportunities.

Social media communities are a good starting point. For example, most B2B companies have listings on LinkedIn, along with many of their employees. Connecting with them and answering questions and sharing insights is a highly effective way to make an impact. Remember, it's not always about directly targeting your primary personas; sometimes you want to target the influencers who know them.

Other effective ways to engage the buying group include attending industry events like webinars, conferences, and interactive workshops. By engaging with all interested parties on multiple levels and through multiple channels, you can better identify and target the highest-value accounts with the most relevant content.

#47 DETERMINE WHICH BUSINESSES CONSTITUTE HIGH-VALUE ACCOUNTS

Once you have organization-wide alignment in place, it's easier for stakeholders to collaborate and decide together whether an account is a good fit for the business. Then, you can tailor your outreach accordingly.

However, before you begin, it's essential to verify your data. According to the LinkedIn ABM report, 43 percent of marketers claim that identifying the right target accounts is a challenge due to unreliable data.

To overcome this, you should analyze historical data in your CRM and other sources to identify which companies have been the most profitable in the past and have the longest client lifetime value (CLTV). Be sure to engage your sales representatives as well, since they have direct interactions with clients and prospects that give them valuable insight.

Enrich what you've learned with intent data. Accounts that have previously demonstrated high engagement rates are often prime targets for ABM. Combining these insights will help you pinpoint the accounts most likely to yield the best results. Finally, based on your findings, define a required list of ICP factors, and establish this as a baseline for identifying high-value accounts.

#48 INCORPORATE ABM INTO USER EXPERIENCE AND CLIENT EXPERIENCE

What makes ABM so effective is its laser focus on highly qualified buyers and buying groups. The process is deeply rooted in client centricity, real-time engagement, and a holistic approach to marketing communications.

Account-based experience (ABX) takes these factors into consideration by incorporating client and user experience (CX and UX) to emphasize the entire experience that accounts have with your business. It's a step above ABM, but one that can help you generate a more engaging, relevant, and targeted experience.

ABX should consider the fact that, on average, 83 percent of buyers spend their time considering a purchase before they even engage with a sales representative. During that time, they're likely to be engaging with content from blog posts to white papers, watching product demonstrations, joining webinars, or signing up for free trials.

Perhaps the biggest challenge is the fact that different accounts engage with a brand in many different ways. Because of this, it's important to standardize the buyer journey as much as possible, albeit while retaining a personalized approach. Be sure to segment communications based on the individual needs of each persona within a buying group, with the overarching goal of moving them seamlessly through their buying journey.

#49 CURATE SOLUTIONS AND SERVICES TO MEET SPECIFIC BUYER NEEDS

ABX requires solutions that are custom tailored to best meet the needs of buyers. After all, curation adds relevance to what would otherwise be a generic offer and forgettable experience. The goal is to eliminate any friction during the buyer journey by having solutions you can adjust by adding or removing features. For example, a SaaS vendor offering accounting software might curate solutions tailored to the unique needs of different business sizes, industries, and geographic locations.

Curation is especially important for software companies, where it's essential to avoid the so-called "feature creep." Customized product demonstrations tailored to the needs of the target account will help you ensure everything remains relevant. If you're using the same approach with everyone, however, you'll end up wasting time showcasing features and solutions that aren't of interest to the target persona.

Effective curation requires quality data, namely behavioral, firmographic, and technographic data associated with target accounts. Delve into historical data from existing clients to learn how others engage with your solutions. Engaging in direct conversations, launching client surveys, and having Q&A sessions after webinars are also effective tactics for gaining a better understanding of how clients use your products.

#50 PLAN CUSTOM-TAILORED THOUGHT LEADERSHIP CONTENT

When sales interactions do occur, it's imperative that they're built on a foundation of perceived value and trust. That means starting with custom-tailored thought leadership content promoted in places where buyers are naturally consuming professional content.

Traditionally, thought leadership encourages marketers to think about the buyer journey from the top of the funnel downward. This involves publishing a broad variety of content designed to raise awareness before shifting to consideration and conversion stages. That's still an important part of any comprehensive marketing strategy but casting such a wide net isn't likely to get you the best clients in short order.

ABM takes a different approach, since it bypasses the awareness stage. Instead, the entire emphasis is on accounts your team have already identified as qualified prospects. This inverted marketing funnel makes highly targeted thought leadership content all the more important. For example, you might have a welcome email or landing page that encourages people to share what they're most interested in learning about. Then, you can serve up exactly the right content and start building meaningful relationships.

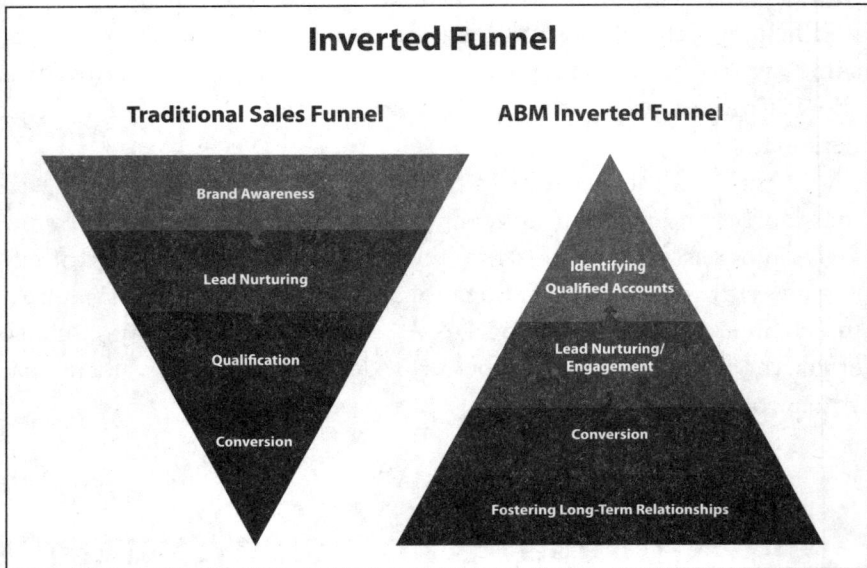

Inverted Funnel

Traditional Sales Funnel

- Brand Awareness
- Lead Nurturing
- Qualification
- Conversion

ABM Inverted Funnel

- Identifying Qualified Accounts
- Lead Nurturing/ Engagement
- Conversion
- Fostering Long-Term Relationships

#51 REVIEW AND UPDATE YOUR STRATEGY AND ADJUST YOUR CRITERIA

Success in ABM hinges on your ability to learn, adapt, and refine your strategy. Whether you're celebrating a win or going through a setback, each outcome offers a lesson. As markets evolve and buyers drop out of the consideration stage, sometimes unexpectedly, you'll need to review how you define your marketing qualified accounts (MQAs). After all, as markets shift and challenges change, so too can the criteria that once defined your MQAs.

Most importantly, the methods you use to collect data on your target accounts can make or break your ABM strategy. When technology advances, new data collection methods emerge, and old ones cease to be as effective as they once were. Always augment and verify your first-party data with trusted third-party sources, and don't rely solely on the existing data in your CRM and other platforms.

When it comes to celebrating wins, don't just focus on replicating them. It's just as important to understand *why* a campaign succeeded, whether it was due to the messaging, the platform, the timing, or something else. Gaining a granular view of your successes lets you continuously refine your strategy for even better results in the future.

The same goes for failures, which, while disappointing, can offer some of the most valuable insights of all. Perhaps a particular message didn't resonate, or you were reaching out to the wrong people. By understanding what didn't work, you can pivot and avoid making the same mistakes.

#52 BUILD A TECH STACK THAT CAN SCALE ACCOUNT-BASED MARKETING

An ABX strategy is undoubtedly costly and difficult to implement, simply because there are so many moving parts. However, the effort is very much worthwhile. You can mitigate these issues by consolidating your tech stack and removing unnecessary software and poor-quality data sources.

Address any bottlenecks first. In many cases, these will be technology-related. For example, you might manage client relationships using your CRM but have a completely separate tool for email marketing or social media outreach. Similarly, your social listening tool might not be compatible with your CRM, thus creating a bottleneck whereby some stakeholders lack access to the data they need to qualify leads and accounts. To provide a cohesive and personalized buyer experience, it stands to reason that your internal processes must also be similarly integrated.

Next, be sure to eliminate any technology bloat where possible. A lean and agile tech stack ensures teams can work easily together without being sidetracked by irrelevant features and data sources. The best ABM tech stacks rely heavily on automated workflows, including list-building features, in-market scoring systems, and targeted advertising tools. Needless to say, the tech stack should span all client-facing departments to stop silos from forming between teams.

#53 USE INTENT AS AN ASSET WITH AN ABM PLATFORM

Intent data, when viewed at the account level, is an incredibly powerful tool for guiding ABM strategies. While individual intent data offers insights for one-to-one personalization and lead nurturing, aggregating the data at the account level helps you scale ABM. For example, if a company identifies multiple individuals in a target account searching for "cloud migration solutions" or attending webinars on the subject, that's a strong indication that the organization might be considering making the move to the cloud.

In another example, let's consider a B2B SaaS vendor that targets companies in the finance sector. If there are several decision-makers in the firm looking for "financial software compliance," then that's a clear sign that they're looking to address a specific pain point. For the seller, this represents a great opportunity to start offering solutions and case studies relevant to compliance challenges.

By focusing on accounts that display high intent, ABM teams can greatly boost their chances of conversion. Accounts that consistently demonstrate intent often yield better conversion rates. However, it's important to cross-reference data with multiple sources to ensure you're targeting the right accounts and individuals.

You can also discover new ABM opportunities by tracking intent data across industries. For instance, if there's a surge in interest in telehealth solutions in the health-care sector, it might signal a broader industry trend.

#54 ADOPT MULTI-THREADING STRATEGIES TO ENGAGE MULTIPLE BUYING GROUP MEMBERS AT ONCE

As frequently evidenced by research, B2B buying processes continue to become more complex, a phenomenon that is both the driver and result of the steadily increasing number of members involved in buying groups.

Consequently, more roles have been incorporated into these groups. The percentage of associates and other low-seniority employees integrating into buying groups has almost doubled between 2024 and 2025, while the number of managers influencing purchase decisions has also increased significantly.

These new members are usually the youngest and the most tech-savvy among influencers and have their own unique concerns and objections when considering a purchase. As these team members are quite often the end users, they can hold significant influence over the buying process. Although C-suite executives and directors/VPs are still responsible for core decision-making, engaging only the highest-level contacts in an account has become an outdated practice.

Marketers must therefore strive to develop communication addressing many different aspects of a solution, including the financial, operational, and strategic benefits relevant to major stakeholders. In order to engage the entirety of the buying group, this should also encompass both the technical and practical criteria constituting the main concern of IT professionals and end users.

#55 LEVERAGE ABX FRAMEWORKS

Account-based experience (ABX), an approach designed to meet specific needs across the buying group, is rooted in delivering highly personalized outreach that resonates with the unique necessities of each influencer. Given the expectation of buyers for seamless, personalized buying experiences, ABX has grown in popularity as a means to establish meaningful connections with multiple buying group members.

For this strategy to be successful, it is crucial to accurately identify the roles of each decision-maker, both within the company as a whole and in the buying process specifically.

Next, strive to identify the broader pain points multiple buying group members can relate to. This is usually linked to a bottom-line goal, such as driving sales or increasing productivity, and will be the most relevant aspect for high-level decision-makers.

Finally, break these broad objectives down into specific objectives that enable each role to contribute toward the end goal. For example, task management software can help take some pressure off low-seniority employees by organizing clearer timelines and task priorities and creating more time for strategic work. On the other hand, managers can benefit from that same software by earning actionable insights into their team's efforts. Both aspects ultimately contribute to boosting overall productivity (the C-suite's end goal).

Now, your ABM campaign is informed by each influencer's unique pain points, and, by delivering content in their preferred channels and formats, all buying group members can enjoy a highly personalized experience, without losing sight of the purchase's overarching goal.

CHAPTER 5

CREATING CONTENT THAT CONVERTS

It might come as a surprise that content marketing is more lucrative than ever. But, according to a 2023 survey by the Content Marketing Institute, 71 percent of respondents claimed it was even more important than the previous year.

Despite this, around half of B2B decision-makers are bored by B2B marketing content. Given the rapidly increasing prevalence of content in this space that lacks personality (partially due to misuse of AI), that perhaps shouldn't come as a surprise. The state of content marketing also isn't helped by the fact that a great deal of content exists for SEO only, paying little heed to the actual needs and preferences of human audiences.

It's time for that to change, which is why the number one priority in any content marketing plan should be creating content that converts due to its relevance.

#56 — IMPLEMENT A CONTENT MAP TO ESTABLISH CLEAR GOALS FOR YOUR CONTENT

2024 research from Demand Gen Report states that the majority of buyers feel that most content is too generic and irrelevant to their needs. While this is partially due to the misuse of generative AI systems, the lack of personalization and alignment with buyer needs is in no way a novelty from the AI era.

Although offering prospects a cohesive and highly relevant content experience can pose a daunting challenge, strategies such as content mapping can be leveraged to break this process down into actionable steps. Content maps help you visualize the goals and needs of buyer personas across buying stages. This process can guide the creation of your demand content and inform audits by illustrating the experience offered by your content strategy and shedding light on any potential gaps.

Analyzing your different buyer personas and theorizing their journeys can help you understand the specific function each content piece must play in your overarching content plan. Strive to understand how prospect needs, goals, and pain points evolve and aim to deliver content that offers value, positions your solution favorably, and resolves objections as they arise.

If not done already, your existing content library can then be analyzed against your content map to scope out how your content supports the buying journey of each persona. Remember to iterate and optimize this process as both your content strategy and target audiences evolve.

#57 DEVELOP A STYLE GUIDE TO INFORM CONTENT CREATION

Buyers increasingly demand seamless buying experiences, expecting consistency throughout all communications. Especially in large scale marketing approaches such as omnichannel and multichannel strategies, ensuring this consistency becomes key to building a compelling brand-to-demand experience.

Therefore, companies must strive to ensure their on- and offline presence is cohesive, supporting a homogenous identity across different channels. In the same way that brand guidelines ensure the consistency of design and bolster brand identity, writing style guides can be invaluable resources to ensure written materials contribute to a compelling brand experience.

Elements such as tone, formality, and content length can all be ingredients to express your unique identity in writing. Well-defined writing style guides align content creation according to the same quality standards, ensuring your brand's unique identity and voice come through in all touchpoints, contributing to a seamless experience.

#58 DEVELOP THOUGHT LEADERSHIP CONTENT TO MEET BUYERS WHERE THEY ARE

A quick glance at the average business blog or social media page makes it clear that a lot of content doesn't go beyond the awareness stage of the buyer journey, existing mainly to gain traction in search results. While no one can deny the importance of raising awareness through SEO/GEO/AEO, B2B buyers in particular tend to be more interested in relevance and thought leadership. If your content doesn't demonstrate your organization's expertise in its space, then it's unlikely to drive conversions.

Thought leadership content goes beyond awareness alone to engage prospects throughout each stage of the buyer journey. Here are some examples of what a winning content marketing funnel should look like:

- **Awareness:** Top-of-funnel (TOFU) content includes highly shareable blog posts, social media posts, infographics, and video content. It serves to get prospects through the door and interested enough to learn more.
- **Evaluation:** Middle-of-funnel (MOFU) content includes white papers, case studies, and email newsletters. Its goal is to turn prospects into potential buyers by demonstrating why they should choose your product over others.
- **Conversion:** At the bottom of the funnel (BOFU), the goal should be to build upon your MOFU content with clear calls to action, free trials, and product demonstrations.

- **Advocacy:** Contrary to popular belief, a content strategy isn't all about marketing, but also about nurturing existing clients with content that helps them get more out of your products and services.

Thought leadership should ideally span the entire content marketing funnel but it's important to tailor your strategy in a way that it reaches the right people at the right time. For example, you might share blogs intended primarily to raise awareness on social media, and your latest white papers and case studies with prospects who have already provided their email contacts.

#59 DEVELOP BUYER-LED CONTENT

As a result of the saturation of low-quality AI-generated content, the percentage of buyers who consider most content generic and irrelevant has shown an uptick of 13 percent from 2023 to 2024. Shockingly, although 72 percent of content marketers report utilizing generative AI, 61 percent say they have no guidelines for its usage, according to 2024 research by the Content Marketing Institute. This adds to the ongoing misalignment between buyer needs and marketers' preferences.

Consequently, the quality of content and its role in enabling seamless buying experiences have since become a core focus in content strategies. Buyer-led content strives to incorporate these aspects into content creation from the very beginning.

Buyer-led content strategies involve in-depth analysis of your audience's behavior, preferences, and pain points, enabling your campaigns to meet their needs with high precision. Feedback from sales teams can also help marketers understand the role played by content in different stages of the buyer's journey, by noting the pieces that supported sales enablement and contributed to closing deals.

In sum, buyer-led content aims to empower prospects with resources to easily navigate complex decisions, de-risking your solutions by cementing trust in your brand and solutions by providing value at all touchpoints.

#60 UTILIZE RESPONSIVE DESIGN FOR MOBILE USERS

More than half of all web traffic originates from mobile devices, and B2B users spend more time on their smartphones and tablets than ever before. Whether they're reading the latest industry news on the daily commute or tapping through social media updates, chances are they're on the small screen. Therefore, it's vital to cater to mobile users when planning the layout of your website and its content.

Responsive design retrieves information like the end user's screen resolution and orientation to automatically adjust on-page elements for a better user experience. This is especially vital for lead capture pages, online surveys, and any other content that has interactive elements. It also helps improve visual appeal and makes your content more comfortable to view.

To drive engagement on mobile devices, you shouldn't stop at responsive design. You also need to ensure your content is suitably formatted for the small screen. Think short, scannable paragraphs with plenty of subheadings, bullet lists, large text, and clear formatting. After all, no one wants to read a massive wall of text on a tiny screen, which makes it crucial to break all content down into bite-size chunks of information, equipped with navigational elements.

Marketers should also consider the mobile friendliness of gated assets like white papers, which are often in downloadable PDF format. The problem with these documents is they have a fixed layout, and they can't easily be tracked or measured. Instead, consider using interactive web-based alternatives powered by HTML5 or JavaScript.

#61 INFORM CONTENT CREATION WITH RELEVANT DATA AND TRENDS

To ensure your content strikes the right chord with your target audience, it must be informed by data-driven insights and current industry trends. If it's not, it will appear out of touch with the needs and preferences of its intended viewers.

There are two main sources of data for informing your content strategy. Firstly, we have buyer intent data. As explored with ABM, this includes buyer activity that indicates interest in a brand, product, or service. It also helps you evaluate people's propensity to make a purchase. That way, you can craft content for ideal touchpoints that engage buying groups at specific stages of their buying journeys. For example, if people are searching for a term like "comparison of email marketing platforms," then they're probably almost ready to purchase. Social listening is ideal for monitoring intent and tracking trends, and no B2B company should be without it.

Another important source of information is the sales team. After all, your sales representatives have direct interaction with your clients, which means they might have insights that other data doesn't capture effectively. Be sure to set up regular meetings with your sales team, ideally weekly, and develop content strategies that align with current priorities and feedback. You can also conduct a strengths, weaknesses, opportunities, and threats (SWOT) analysis to identify key focus areas.

#62 ENSURE CREATIVITY STAYS AT THE FOREFRONT OF YOUR CAMPAIGNS

In many ways, effective marketing is a form of art. And, like any art, its intent is to inspire an emotional reaction. However, that's not likely to happen if your focus is on quantity rather than quality. In the era of generative AI, that's even more poignant.

Also, avoid placing too great an emphasis on SEO. Instead, you should focus on creating marketing collateral that truly aligns with and makes a real and meaningful impact on your audience. Overreliance on automation, especially when it comes to content creation, can end up stifling creativity and diluting your brand message with a dry and generic voice.

Of course, getting creative is often easier said than done, especially for writers, marketers, and designers who are under pressure to keep up with the enormous demand for compelling content. That's why it's always important to find a time and place for creative thinking and to stay alert for inspiration, both in the on- and offline worlds. Be sure to brainstorm whenever an idea comes to mind and stay informed by subscribing to popular industry newsletters.

Another proven way to keep creativity on the center stage is to create *with* the client rather than just *for* the client. Clients are themselves creators, specifically of user-generated content like social media posts and reviews. In today's client-centric world, it makes sense to look to clients themselves for inspiration.

#63 INTEGRATE GENERATIVE AI INTO YOUR CONTENT WORKFLOWS

Few innovations have made such a sudden and dramatic impact on marketing as generative AI has in recent years. Today, marketers can generate almost any type of content using AI, whether it's visual content with Midjourney or DALL-E, written content with ChatGPT or Claude, or even video content using Synthesia. The problem is that overreliance on such tools stifles creativity and significantly increases the risks of copyright infringement, plagiarism, and misinformation.

On one extreme are marketers who care only about quantity and are happy to dramatically scale their content output at minimal cost, even if it results in mass-produced, low-quality content that has little chance of increasing conversions. On the other side are the more creatively minded marketers, strategists, writers, and designers who see AI as a way to augment rather than replace. Ultimately, marketers who learn how to leverage AI in an optimal and sustainable manner will win over those who rely on it excessively or eschew it altogether.

Savvy marketers are already adopting generative AI to streamline their workflows and perform better at their jobs. Proven use cases for AI include analyzing trends, brainstorming topic ideas, summarizing content, and analyzing user behavior and preferences. By integrating AI into your content workflows in a thoughtful and strategic manner, you can work smarter.

#64 PRIORITIZE CONTENT RELEVANCE AND AUTHORITY

B2B buyers engage with an average of thirteen pieces of content before choosing a vendor. This includes content created both by the vendor and by third parties, such as reviews and social media. While you don't have any direct control over what others write about your brand or its products, you're solely responsible for ensuring that all the content you publish is relevant to your audience.

The importance of content relevance and authority can't be overstated. In fact, it's arguably even more important than reach. After all, having a thousand users visit a blog post means nothing if almost all of them are bouncing instead of engaging with your content. Ensure your content, including blog posts, white papers, and lead magnet pages, addresses the pain points listed in your client profiles and that it aligns with their psychographic, behavioral, and firmographic traits. Remember, it's much better to make a meaningful impact on a few prospects than it is to try to appeal to as many people as possible.

#65 INVEST IN PILLAR PAGES AND OTHER LONG-FORM CONTENT

Given the typically lengthy and complex sales cycles in B2B, depth and authority are essential for maintaining a healthy conversion rate. Moreover, as the digital landscape becomes more saturated, you need to take extra care to produce content that not only stands out but also serves as a valuable resource for your target audience. That's where long-form content really shines:

- **Pillar pages:** These are long-form blog posts and articles that cover a specific topic in depth. They often serve as the main hub for a particular subject, linking out to related subtopics, including short blog posts and other resources. For example, an information security vendor might have a pillar page dedicated to "enterprise cybersecurity best practices," which then links to more niche topics like "phishing attack prevention" and "multifactor authentication."
- **White papers:** A reliable content format for B2B demand generation, white papers include authoritative reports that delve deep into a specific issue and offer solutions in combination with data insights. For example, a B2B SaaS vendor offering supply chain management solutions might publish a white paper exploring supply chain automation, backed up by data points from reputable sources or proprietary studies. White papers are often gated behind lead capture pages.
- **eBooks:** While similar to white papers and pillar pages in terms of depth, eBooks are typically broader in scope and serve as valuable educational resources. They tend to be concept-centric rather than data-centric and are based on ideas, trends, and areas of interest rather than hard data. They can also be more casual and conversational than white papers and tend to be best suited to the middle of the sales funnel.

Remember that B2B decision-makers are always on the lookout for content that can inform their own choices and strategies. Long-form content pieces that include clear calls to action (CTAs) are crucial to guide readers toward the next steps in their buyer journeys.

#66 ADJUST CONTENT BASED ON FEEDBACK

Feedback can be a gold mine for content marketers, especially in the B2B space. It provides direct insights into what your audience thinks, feels, and needs. But collecting feedback is just the beginning. The real value lies in how you leverage feedback to refine your content strategy.

There are several ways to collect feedback. Among the most comprehensive are client surveys. However, since they take time for people to complete, you'll likely only get a decent response rate from heavy users in your existing client base; incentivization is also often required to encourage responses. For your other prospects and clients, there are quicker and simpler ways to get feedback to inform content strategy. For example, adding a button that allows readers to upvote or downvote content can be effective, as well as simply sharing a list of topics they may be interested in.

Surveys and other sources of feedback help you identify content preferences. If, for example, feedback indicates a preference for more in-depth content over quick reads, then it's probably time to step up your output of white papers and pillar pages.

Furthermore, if you know who's providing the feedback, as you likely will in the case of surveys, you'll be able to match content preferences with specific buyer personas.

More broadly speaking, feedback can also help you spot emerging trends. For instance, if multiple respondents are expressing concerns about a new regulation, that's a cue to produce content that addresses those concerns.

#67 CREATE EDUCATIONAL CONTENT THAT SOLVES PROBLEMS

Great content doesn't just trigger an emotional response. It also solves real-world problems and inspires people to act. Corporate decision-makers face complex challenges when they're aligning solutions with their operational goals. It's essential that your marketing collateral not only communicates the value you can provide but also offers something relevant for free. Here are some examples:

- **Comparison articles** help decision-makers choose between competing products.
- **How-to guides** help existing clients and trial users get more out of your solutions.
- **White papers** provide industry-specific thought leadership and valuable insights.
- **Case studies** demonstrate how your solutions have helped similar clients in the past.
- **Content in various formats** can address knowledge gaps found in specific industries.
- **Knowledge bases and resource centers** establish your brand as an industry authority.

The above list is by no means exhaustive, but it illustrates where the true power of content marketing lies. After all, creating educational content is a proven strategy that's worked for brands for well over a century from recipes on the back of food packaging to industry journals published by household brand names.

By focusing on educational content, you can increase your reach, earn referral traffic, boost conversion rates, and maximize CLTV by turning clients into brand advocates. Ultimately, it's a full-funnel approach that's vastly more powerful than just thinking in terms of keyword-based SEO.

#68 LEVERAGE USER-GENERATED CONTENT FOR GREATER AUTHENTICITY

User-generated content (UGC) is brand-specific or product-specific content created by clients and published on social media, review sites, personal blogs, forums, and various other platforms. The power of

UGC lies in the fact that, unsurprisingly, potential buyers are more likely to trust the word of an existing client than that of the brand itself. As such, UGC has a huge influence on purchase decisions.

The very fact that brands typically don't have direct control over UGC is what makes it more authentic. Of course, that also means there's always the risk of receiving negative feedback in the form of a bad review or a dissatisfied post on social media. However, marketers shouldn't be afraid of bad press, not least because people often put just as much weight into how brands respond to negative feedback than the feedback itself.

Encouraging UGC gives your existing and potential clients a voice and demonstrates that you genuinely care about their opinions. It can also help inform your branded content strategy, manage your reputation more effectively, and build trust.

Proven ways to leverage UGC include asking clients to leave reviews on platforms relevant to your industry, hosting contests and sweepstakes, and using branded social media hashtags. With the added benefit of social listening solutions, you can also track what people are saying about your brand and get involved in the conversation to address any objections or concerns.

#69 INFORM CONTENT WITH INSIGHTS FROM SALES TEAMS

Sales teams are in close contact with prospective buyers as they help them navigate their buying journeys. As such, they have access to invaluable feedback on the specific content topics in demand from specific audience segments. Even if anecdotal, this information can be greatly helpful in developing a comprehensive content plan that caters to the unique needs of your prospects.

Furthermore, analyzing the relationship between content assets leveraged by sales efforts and conversion rates can provide insights into the performance of your content that would otherwise stay in the dark funnel.

Lastly, direct interaction between sales teams and buyers can grant marketers valuable insights into the language clients use when discussing their challenges. Siloed marketers often risk relying on jargon and expressions that fail to resonate with actual buyers. By leaning on sales reps to understand how prospects describe their own needs and pain points, marketers can fuel hyper-relevant outreach that communicates messaging to prospects in the most resonant way.

#70 OFFER PERSONALIZED EXPERIENCES WITH AI-POWERED DYNAMIC WEBSITE CONTENT

As the number of influencers in buying groups steadily increases, with the majority consuming over seven content pieces each throughout their journeys, delivering hyper-relevant content is crucial to stand out.

At the intersection of cutting-edge AI technology, content marketing, and data-driven strategies, dynamic website content is an invaluable tool to offer highly personalized buying experiences. This feature analyzes buyers, buying groups, and account history instantaneously upon page load, presenting the user with content curated to cater to their unique needs.

A content map and data insights on active prospects/accounts are the key ingredients needed to fuel this strategy, fostering a seamless, custom-tailored buying experience in tune with the demands of today's buyers.

CHAPTER 6

HARNESSING THE POWER OF CHANNEL AND PARTNER MARKETING

Channel marketing is the planning and development of strategies across each individual point of contact with prospective and existing clients. The channels you use will vary depending on current trends, audience needs, and business priorities. Strategies can consist of a mix of digital and in-person channels.

To boost channel marketing performance, businesses typically work with channel partners to take advantage of shared audiences. This is especially valuable in highly competitive verticals like technology and software. Examples of channel partnerships include influencers, affiliates, referrals, and co-marketing arrangements.

INFUSE research found that 64 percent of B2B vendors allocate at least half of their budgets to channel partner marketing. It's an undeniably effective strategy for sales and marketing teams seeking to promote value across their partnerships and, in doing so, become more visible in their respective markets.

In this chapter, we'll share some of the best practices for building a channel partner marketing campaign that will help you achieve your business goals.

#71 UNDERSTAND THE TYPES OF CHANNEL PARTNERS

The burgeoning partnership ecosystem is changing the way modern companies do business by creating an environment built on communication and cooperation. Channel partnerships take the center stage in that transformation by helping organizations expand their reach. By choosing channel partners that match your goals and target audience, you can stand out even in the most competitive verticals. However, before you begin, you need to be familiar with the most important types of channel partners in B2B markets:

- **Co-marketing arrangements** are strategic alliances between one or more organizations that share similar goals and target markets but are not competing with one another. For example, if a company offers a cloud-based project management tool and another offers time-tracking software, both could collaborate in the pursuit of similar goals.
- **Influencer partnerships** help you tap into large audiences on social media. Traditionally considered more of a B2C strategy, B2B companies are now leveraging influencers with significant success. Examples include Microsoft partnering with National Geographic to highlight women in STEM careers and IBM leveraging its employees as influencers.
- **Affiliate marketing** involves partnering with media companies to promote products and services. Depending on the arrangement, the affiliate earns a commission for every sale, lead, or click generated. For example, a tech blogger may publish an article about a B2B SaaS product that contains a unique referral link.
- **Referral marketing** is similar to affiliate marketing but instead leverages a company's own clients as advocates rather than an outsider. It's a commonly untapped revenue stream that typically incentivizes the sharing of positive client experiences with others in a specific target market.

Other strategic partnerships that expand sales and marketing reach include distributors and resellers, some of which add value to the original offer by bundling extra services or features. These are especially popular in the SaaS industry. Choosing the right channel partners can significantly amplify a company's market influence, while also ensuring a consistent and high-quality experience for the end client.

#72 SEGMENT YOUR PARTNERS AND MEASURE PERFORMANCE

To harness the full potential of your channel partners, you must categorize them strategically. It's not all about the revenue generated: it's also about aligning strengths, audiences, and performance metrics in a way that helps you predict and influence future results. Here's a breakdown of how to effectively segment your partners:

- **Capabilities first:** Every channel partner brings unique strengths to the table. While one may be a powerhouse of technical knowledge, another might have a foothold in a specific region or industry. Recognizing these capabilities supports a more closely aligned collaboration.
- **Audience alignment:** It's about who your partners know and the sort of people they influence. For example, if a partner has deep connections with businesses and individuals in health care, then they're probably a natural fit for a company offering a SaaS product centered on health care.
- **Metrics matter:** Relevant measurement is critical to determine how the arrangement is going. Regularly monitoring key metrics like revenue generated and conversion rates will help you identify your best-performing channel partners, while also highlighting those who might be falling behind expectations.

When identifying and onboarding new partners, taking a deep dive into their capabilities and audiences is a must. Partner surveys can be a gold mine here, since they help pinpoint the level of support they might need, the marketing development funds (MDF) they would require to achieve the desired results, and which of your programs best align with their strengths.

#73 LEAN ON SMALLER PARTNERS TO TARGET NICHE QUALIFICATION CRITERIA

Channel marketing strategies often overlook smaller channel partners, giving preference to major players with preestablished influence. However, this is to be expected, as vendors seek to achieve performance and meet revenue goals quickly, resulting in larger partners becoming prioritized. Consequently, smaller partners can face increased difficulties due to a lack of resources, know-how, and funding.

While bigger partnerships bring to the table a wider, more general reach, smaller partners offer more specialized, focused targeting. This can help you achieve high levels of resonance, unattainable for companies communicating exclusively with broader audiences.

To ensure success when working with small channel partners, however, it is imperative to provide them with the necessary budget and resources to drive valuable marketing outcomes, such as vendor content. Training sessions and consistent support are also crucial for ensuring your product's differentiators and unique proposals are adequately communicated.

#74 CHOOSE THE RIGHT DEMAND GENERATION PARTNERS

Demand generation is the strategic process of creating interest and engagement in a company's offerings with the goal of building and accelerating pipeline and ultimately driving revenue. It spans the full buyer's journey, from building awareness to generating qualified leads ready for sales handoff. In other words, demand generation helps you gain greater reach and engagement with target audiences by positioning your content in front of the right buyers and answering their questions in a timely manner.

Creating a demand generation strategy begins with choosing the right partner. Paid platforms are typically more effective, however, since they often have rigid quality standards and large networks ready to distribute your content assets to a qualified audience. For example, Outbrain has an impressive distribution network including CNN, MSN, and Sky News. INFUSE also has its own network, ITCurated, which is industry-specific and promotes content to a large audience of B2B profiles worldwide across 35+ verticals.

Having buyer-led, demand-ready content is essential for a successful demand generation strategy. Ask your partners how they plan to promote your brand and your content; whether they have wholly-owned networks or if they rely on third parties or outsources. Each partner has different rules and protocols. For example, some may simply republish your work, while others might edit it down to a shorter version or just link to the full piece with an excerpt. It's important to keep these factors in mind from an SEO/GEO/AEO perspective, since search engines and LLMs typically only rank the original version of the content.

Finally, be sure to establish your success metrics when entering into a partnership. Important metrics include ROI, volume and quality, and traffic.

#75 CONSIDER ENTERING INTO A CO-MARKETING AGREEMENT

A co-marketing agreement between noncompeting companies that nonetheless serve the same target audiences can be extremely effective for expanding reach and building authority. This is especially the case with disruptive startups wanting to find a viable market fit for new and innovative solutions that have few or no equals.

Co-marketing arrangements may collaborate on content creation or even go so far as bundling multiple related products together to add value. Some partnerships, especially in B2B SaaS, may even lead to deeper business relationships, potentially paving the way for discussions on new investment and acquisition opportunities.

Co-marketing campaigns require extensive partner research. Potential partnerships must be thoroughly vetted to ensure both sides of the deal are maintained and that your brand image doesn't end up being damaged by negative association. As such, the best partnerships involve brands with closely aligned missions, values, and target audiences.

Solid collaborations can also be highly beneficial to end clients. For example, in the B2B SaaS space, integration across different software products is a major priority among decision-makers. Two or more companies coming together to market their solutions can help address this common pain point, while also allowing both parties to tap into a broader market.

When looking for co-marketing partners, be sure they have an active presence on social media, a rock-solid brand reputation, and a strong voice in the market. Finally, as with demand generation or any other partnership, make sure you create a comprehensive plan for tracking and assessing your campaign's performance.

#76   INVEST IN HIGH-VALUE GUEST BLOGGING OPPORTUNITIES

It's been a decade since Google's former head of web spam claimed guest blogging is dead. What he was really taking aim at, however, were the low-quality affiliate blog posts and article marketing methods that were popular at the time. Although the same problems persist to this day, guest blogging yields impressive results when performed strategically.

As with any form of digital marketing, quality is paramount. Focus on relevant guest blogging opportunities with industry-specific blogs and consistently publish value-driven content. While the bar to entry might be higher, that's exactly what maintains higher standards. Also, be wary of paid guest blogging opportunities, unless they involve well-known media sites with high domain authorities. Guest blogging is meant to be a mutually beneficial arrangement, whereby the blog owner usually profits from valuable content for free, while the individual or company producing it gains exposure.

Leverage existing relationships by proactively reaching out to other bloggers and influencers in your niche. This can strengthen your network and lead to further backlinking opportunities. When contacting blog owners for the first time, whether via social media or email, personalize your outreach using open-ended templates. Be sure to show genuine interest in their work by mentioning a specific piece of content you like from their website.

#77 HOLD REMOTE, HYBRID, AND IN-PERSON EVENTS

Events play an important role in channel marketing, since they help expand your network and foster valuable business relationships. This, in turn, helps you increase brand visibility and drive sales. This is why the value of in-person events must not be overlooked, even with the rising popularity of online and hybrid events.

Popular event formats include trade shows and exhibitions that allow companies to showcase their offerings to potential clients and partners. Workshops and training sessions are another option, offering a more intimate setting where businesses can nurture partners with the knowledge and skills they need to sell or support their products and services. These events may also include live demos.

Partner conferences and summits tend to be larger and more focused, bringing together stakeholders from across the channel ecosystem to offer networking opportunities, breakout discussions, and keynote sessions. For example, a B2B SaaS company might host a partner conference to delve into the new features of their latest product release. Including hands-on training and workshops can equip channel partners with the knowledge they need to address client challenges and common objections.

Most events can also take place in remote or hybrid environments. This is ideal for companies that have partners spread over a large geographic region or serve multiple countries. Each format has its pros and cons, so be sure to carefully evaluate them in terms of your specific objectives before deciding.

#78 LEVERAGE YOUR WEBSITE AS A CHANNEL HUB

As the digital storefront for your business, the end goal of any marketing channel is to drive traffic to your website. Whether it's guest blogging, co-marketing, influencer marketing, or any other strategy, your proprietary website should serve as a central hub for channel and partner marketing.

Take the time to create a user experience that encourages visitors to stay on the site for longer and consume more content. Relevance and quality are vital here. For example, if someone visits your website via a referral or guest blog post, then it's imperative that they can continue their journey to find what they're looking for. Remember, it's not about driving traffic for its own sake, but boosting relevant traffic.

As for partner marketing, consider setting up a dedicated partner portal on your website. This can give partners easy access to critical resources like marketing collateral, training materials, sales tools, and product updates. By centralizing these assets, you can ensure channel partners have the latest information they need to represent your brand consistently and effectively.

By adding comprehensive website analytics into the mix, you can also get a granular view of the journey both channel partners and potential clients take when visiting your website. This can help reveal gaps in information, identify which products generate the most interest, and pinpoint where that traffic comes from.

#79 REPURPOSE CONTENT FOR DIFFERENT CHANNELS

Optimizing content for demand generation requires tailoring it for different channels. Each channel in your strategy appeals to different market segments and audience personas. For example, some prospects prefer bite-size information presented via infographics, especially at the top of the sales funnel. Others, particularly in the middle of the funnel, prefer deeper content, such as white papers and case studies.

Different channels favor not only specific content types but also different stages of the sales funnel. To get the most mileage out of your content, repurpose it for the appropriate channel or partner. Long-form content such as white papers, case studies, and eBooks can be edited down into more digestible formats. Conversely, you can elaborate on a popular guest post that's driving a lot of traffic to your website by using it as the basis for a pillar post or other long-form piece.

Many channel partners, such as guest bloggers and influencers, have strict content standards and formats. That's not to say they'll necessarily reject the content you give them on grounds of quality or relevance, but they too may be looking for consistency or specific content formats. For instance, if you have a popular infographic getting lots of shares on social media, capitalizing on its popularity by publishing it on a major media outlet can be a powerful strategy. Although media outlets may only accept articles and blog posts, it's still much easier and cheaper to repurpose existing content into these formats if necessary.

#80 TAP INTO THE POWER OF INDUSTRY INFLUENCERS

Partnering with industry influencers offers an effective way to reach your audience where they already are. Though traditionally associated with B2C markets, finding influential key players in B2B industries with large social media followings almost guarantees exposure.

To identify the right influencers, you need to find those with target audiences similar to your own and at the same stage of the buying journey you're targeting. For example, if your goal is to raise awareness, then social media influencers with large industry-specific networks are suitable. However, if you're targeting prospects further down the funnel, who are actively looking for a solution, you should seek out influencers like professional reviewers who collate or aggregate solutions for your industry.

An easy way to source influencers is by searching for industry-specific hashtags on LinkedIn. For certain industries, this can also work on X or Instagram. Reach out to the authors and publishers of relevant content and ask them if they'd be interested in partnership opportunities, such as sponsored content or guest posting.

Alternatively, you can leverage your internal team as B2B influencers. This can be especially powerful for larger businesses with subject matter experts who also have their own followings on social media or their own blogs. Company executives, for instance, tend to have large networks of people in similar roles and industries. They too can serve as brand advocates and further expand the reach of your campaigns.

#81 ENABLE PARTNER THOUGHT LEADERSHIP WITH HIGH-QUALITY CONTENT

As today's defensive buyers emphasize the need to de-risk purchase decisions, social proof and unbiased third-party validation become crucial to fostering the trust necessary for them to complete a purchase. Consequently, gone is the time when buyers reached out to partners exclusively in the transactional stages of the buying process.

With roughly two out of three buyers now relying on the channel ecosystem to inform their purchases, vendors encounter novel opportunities to impact new markets and drive growth. When equipped with the right resources and properly trained on your product's unique selling points, channel partners can leverage thought leadership content as a pivotal asset to offer end users the validation they need.

As partners seek to consolidate their reputation, establish trust, and develop closer relationships with clients, they find the need to craft more thought leadership content. However, partners often lack the resources and budgets at the disposal of vendors. This is where you come in: providing partners with hard research data that resonates with your shared audiences, for example, enables them to craft effective thought leadership content. Such content, in turn, fosters buyer trust and drives demand for your partners. When the time comes to actually market your solutions through them, their audiences are thus primed to receive your shared messaging.

#82 EXPLORE YOUR AFFILIATE MARKETING OPTIONS

Working with affiliates is another proven way to leverage partnerships to elevate your channel marketing. While often questioned in B2B, working with the right affiliates willing to feature ads and other content on their websites can offer a more targeted approach than many forms of paid advertising. That said, payment structures are typically similar, with affiliates being paid for each click on a referral link.

In B2B, the emphasis is on building long-term relationships through relevant partnerships and content designed to convert, rather than simply generating traffic. That's why it's vital to partner with reputable affiliates who have a credible reputation in your industry. For example, a B2B SaaS company may work with a well-regarded industry blogger or niche consultancy firm to promote their brands and services.

Since B2B purchases are typically more complex and require a deeper understanding of the product and the challenges it addresses, be sure to give your affiliates ample information about your solution and offer them competitive commissions. Finally, use tracking and analytics to measure the performance of your campaigns, but ensure your affiliates are transparent and willing to disclose the arrangement. Doing so is essential for preserving and building trust and authenticity.

#83 SET UP PROCESSES TO MOTIVATE EXISTING CLIENTS TO PROVIDE REFERRALS

In B2B, it's often clients who are your most valuable potential partners. Start by identifying the clients with the highest lifetime value, since this likely demonstrates a high level of satisfaction with your product. Be sure to leverage incentivization and facilitate the process of clients sharing their experiences. Referral marketing is enormously effective, simply because B2B decision-makers are far more likely to base their purchase decisions on what existing clients have to say about a brand or product.

Referral marketing depends on offering exceptional client service and user experience, so if you already have perfected those assets, you're halfway through to winning clients with referrals. Ideally, referral programs should be hard-baked into the client experience. For example, many B2B companies offer incentives to clients who refer others. These incentives are usually financial, such as credit toward subscription renewals for both the referrer and the client being referred.

While this automated and integrated approach can help you scale referral marketing across your entire client base, the most valuable referrals tend to come from the clients with the highest CLTV. For instance, a satisfied client who's been with you for years and whose account has been enormously valuable to your company is a prime candidate for top-quality referrals. Moreover, they might also be willing to be interviewed for a client case study or success story, both of which are proven to be among the most effective B2B content formats of all.

#84 ASSESS YOUR PARTNER PERFORMANCE REGULARLY

Forging high-value partnerships has never been more important, especially during periods of economic uncertainty. To succeed, you need partners who are transparent, data-driven, agile, and forward-thinking. The ideal partners will have strong relationships with their audiences and the ability to identify and tap into the buying groups that matter most.

Ensure your channel partner marketing strategy aligns with your own business goals. If you're aiming to break into new markets, for instance, you need partners with strong footholds in those areas. Other important factors when assessing the performance of existing or potential channel partners include:

- **Financial health:** The economic resilience of your channel partners has both direct and indirect effects on your broader marketing campaign and brand recognition. Working with partners who are lagging behind financially can give your company a poor image.
- **Technological readiness:** The dynamic nature of the digital landscape requires regular review of your channel partners' ability to accommodate the needs of potential buyers. After all, it won't look good if your marketing content is appearing on outdated websites, and this will also likely impact their ability to track performance.
- **Training and enablement:** Equipping your partners with the tools and knowledge they need to promote your services may require time and other resources, but it's essential for

businesses with more complex solutions or buying cycles. It's imperative that your partners fully understand and believe in what they're promoting.

- **Performance metrics:** Establish key performance indicators (KPIs) for all your partners and regularly review and update them to ensure they're relevant to your current goals. Finally, ensure your KPIs are communicated across all parties in the arrangement to keep everyone on the same page and working toward the same goals.

Remember, assessing your B2B channel partners should be an ongoing, data-driven process. This demands continuous monitoring, transparent communication, and the ability to adapt to evolving market needs and feedback from partners and clients alike.

#85 PROVIDE TRAINING AND DATA INSIGHTS FOR YOUR PARTNERS

Even the most well-established partners can benefit greatly from shared insights and resources that help them drive demand and build connections. Consider scheduling recurring meetings and training sessions to keep your partners up to date with the topics, pain points, and goals that resonate the most with your buyers.

Sharing audience and campaign data insights with one another is also a beneficial strategy to boost the efficiency of marketing initiatives from vendors and channel partners alike. Therefore, establishing a flow of data insights with your partners can not only empower them to market your solutions more effectively but also inform your product development and go-to-market strategies.

PART THREE

NURTURING LEADS AND CLOSING DEALS

Like personal relationships, business relationships depend on mutual understanding, trust, and responsiveness. If you don't work on them, the positive feelings will eventually wane, no matter how well they started. That's where nurturing comes in.

In part 2, we delved into the various tactics for generating interest in your products and solutions. But that's just half of the job done. To close the deal, you need to nurture your buyers and buying groups by being persistent without being insistent, and strategic rather than haphazard.

Nurturing is all about building lasting relationships, so it's essential to take a long-term view that goes beyond closing deals. After all, the clients with the highest CLTV tend to be brand advocates. They're the ones who keep returning or renewing their subscriptions thanks to the seamless transition from marketing to sales to client experience and support.

In part 3, we'll explore what it takes to build a high-performing nurturing process that helps reengage buyers, shorten sales cycles, and contribute to higher conversion rates throughout the buying journey. We'll also take a deep dive into funnel optimization strategies, cultivating relationships, and aligning your internal teams to deliver a superlative client experience.

CHAPTER 7

OPTIMIZING SALES FUNNELS FOR MAXIMUM CONVERSIONS

In B2B marketing, the sales funnel stands as a testament to a brand's ability to guide potential clients from awareness to advocacy. But it's not just about getting leads into the funnel in the first place; it's also about ensuring they transition through each stage smoothly, ultimately culminating in a sales deal. That journey is unique for each prospect, audience persona, and company, hence it demands meticulous attention to detail.

The traditional sales funnel has served us well, but as B2B industries evolve, so too must our strategies. Average conversion rates for paid search, for example, currently stand at just over 2 percent, while the top 10 percent have an average of 11.7 percent. Moreover, very few B2B prospects will convert following the first engagement. In fact, 80 percent of conversions only come after five or more follow-ups after the first contact, and yet only 8 percent of sales reps follow up this many times.

In this chapter, we'll look into the many nuances of the sales funnel, from fine-tuning your qualification criteria to creating impactful touchpoints tailored to your audience's needs. By optimizing every stage of the sales funnel under a common goal, our aim is to enhance the client experience and ensure that every interaction counts.

#86   EMPHASIZE BUYER ENABLEMENT OVER SALES-LED JOURNEYS

B2B buyers are subject to increased pressure to deliver ROI on their purchases, resulting in slower and more defensive and scrutinous buying processes. Consequently, by the point most prospects reach out to sales representatives, 85 percent of them will already have determined their specific requirements for the purchase and narrowed down their primary vendor options.

For this reason, sales-led journeys and funnel models are falling out of sync with the market's demands. To best cater to the modern buyer's requirements, early funnel stages must focus predominantly on enabling buyer-led research rather than prescribing a set buyer's journey down the funnel.

Content is now sought by prospective buyers to help them navigate increasingly complex purchase decisions. Sales representatives must also be equipped with the assets and knowledge necessary to support the buying process, de-risk your solutions, facilitate decision-making, and resolve objections as they arise.

#87   UNDERSTAND THE DIFFERENCE BETWEEN MQLs AND SQLs

Understanding the difference between marketing qualified leads (MQLs) and sales qualified leads (SQLs) is vital for building a cohesive nurturing strategy. Each category represents a different stage in a potential buyer's journey, and knowing how they differ will significantly impact conversion rates and overall sales performance.

A lead is a broad term referring to any business opportunity, including those identified by your marketing team, that hasn't yet engaged with your brand beyond submitting their contact details. However, once a prospective buyer interacts with your marketing materials or exhibits any behaviors that align with your predefined criteria (as well as ICP criteria), they become an MQL.

Exactly what constitutes a prospective buyer qualified varies by company, but the overarching goal is always the same: ensuring you focus your efforts on the most promising buyers and buying groups as they progress through their buying journey. For example, while a web page visit could be a touchpoint for a prospective buyer, downloading a product-focused white paper might elevate them to MQL status.

SQLs represent a more advanced stage. They're the buyers who have been nurtured by your marketing team over an extended period and meet the criteria necessary to pass them on to the sales team. As prospects who've shown a consistent interest in a brand's offerings, they've undergone a rigorous assessment to ensure they align with your ICPs.

In the complex B2B purchase cycles, buyers and buying groups might remain in the MQL stage for several months, continuously engaging with marketing content. However, only after a thorough evaluation and confirmation of their fit with your ICPs, as well as sustained brand interest ascertained by their engagement, will they be ready to graduate to SQL status.

Understanding these differences and clearly defining the criteria for MQLs and SQLs ensures your marketing efforts stay on target and that your sales team doesn't waste time chasing buyers who aren't likely to convert.

#88 FINE-TUNE YOUR MQL CRITERIA ACCORDING TO BUSINESS NEEDS

Since you'll likely spend several months nurturing your MQLs, it stands to reason that the way you define them significantly influences the efficiency of the lead nurturing process. It ensures that your resources don't go to waste and that you're only targeting prospects who have a real chance of converting. Moreover, changing markets demand a dynamic, adaptable approach that aligns with current business needs and client behaviors.

Start by aligning your sales, marketing, and operations teams. They'll need to work together to establish a shared understanding of what constitutes an MQL. This will ensure that criteria reflects both the insights from your marketing and the firsthand experiences of your sales team. Your operations team will likely be responsible for managing the lead scoring process and nurturing strategies, which is why they also need to be involved.

Demographic, technographic, and firmographic data all play an important role in qualifying leads as MQLs. However, you need to go beyond the basic data points to build a more complete picture. For example, a prospective buyer might fit the demographic profile but might lack the technical know-how or infrastructure required for a suitable market fit. By integrating technographic data into the MQL scoring process, you can ensure they not only have interest but are also capable of adopting your product or service.

Predictive lead scoring is another powerful tool. Analyze past interactions and conversions to assign scores based on historical data. For example, if past conversions show high engagement with a particular webinar, prioritizing buyers who show similar engagement patterns could be an effective strategy. However, given the dynamic nature of B2B marketing, it's important not to implement predictive lead scoring in isolation. Instead, integrate it into the broader process to gain a clearer understanding of the buyers and buying groups you want to nurture.

#89 IDENTIFY AND TRACK INVISIBLE BUYERS IN THE DARK FUNNEL

When buyers drop out of the consideration, it can be difficult to determine why. The problem with the traditional sales funnel is that it doesn't accurately account for buyer behavior from awareness to conversion. This is especially the case in the era of privacy compliance enforced by legislation like the GDPR and CCPA, where tracking online behavior is significantly harder.

That's where the dark funnel comes in. It presents a way to fill the data gaps that arise when specific interactions aren't tracked by analytics platforms. This encompasses the anonymous touchpoints and interactions that prospects have with your brand before they officially begin their buying journey. Typical dark funnel activities may include prospects asking coworkers about your product in person or on a private messaging platform or viewing posts about your product on social media. In a privacy-first world, website visits can't be easily attributed either.

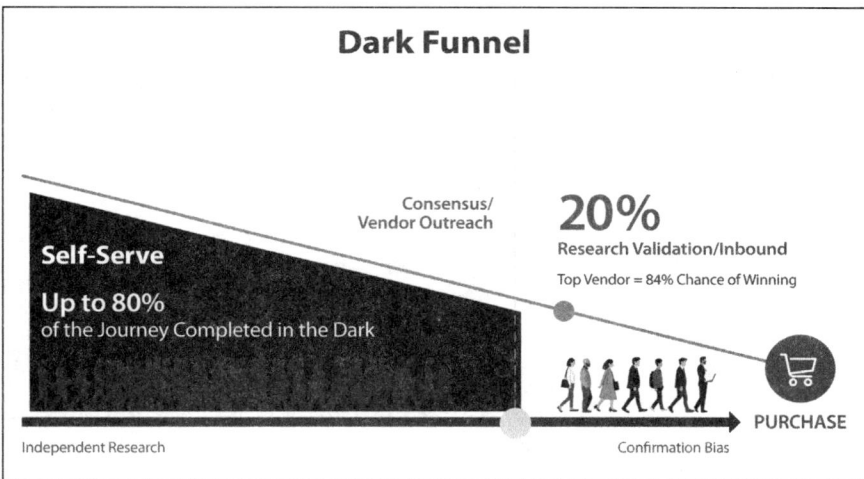

Dark Funnel

Self-Serve

Up to 80%
of the Journey Completed in the Dark

Consensus/
Vendor Outreach

20%
Research Validation/Inbound

Top Vendor = 84% Chance of Winning

PURCHASE

Independent Research

Confirmation Bias

While there's obviously no way to track these touchpoints directly, you can use the data that is available to help fill the gaps. Start by filtering direct traffic on your analytics platform. A lot of "dark traffic" appears as direct on platforms like Google Analytics. This includes web pages that have been memorized or bookmarked. That said, a lot of direct traffic going to a particular page is often a good sign, since it suggests those people have visited before or have been influenced by peers sharing your content via other private channels like instant messaging.

Social media sharing is one of the main sources of dark traffic. However, you can mitigate this by optimizing your content for sharing, such as by adding user-friendly social sharing buttons to each page. Social listening tools used to track brand mentions and branded keywords can also help you logically attribute dark traffic. For instance, if a blog post shared by an influencer is quickly followed by an influx of traffic, you can deduce that it probably originated from their audience.

#90 CONSIDER ALTERNATIVE MODELS TO THE TRADITIONAL SALES FUNNEL

The traditional sales funnel has served us well for over a century, but it's now being challenged by new perspectives that better align with the evolving B2B buyer's journey. Forward-thinking businesses are now exploring alternative models to supplement the sales funnel, such as the following:

- **The AIDA model:** This model helps companies identify the events that occur between the time a prospect learns about a product and when they decide to make a purchase. It encompasses four steps (Attention, Interest, Desire, and Action), which broadly align with those of the traditional sales funnel.

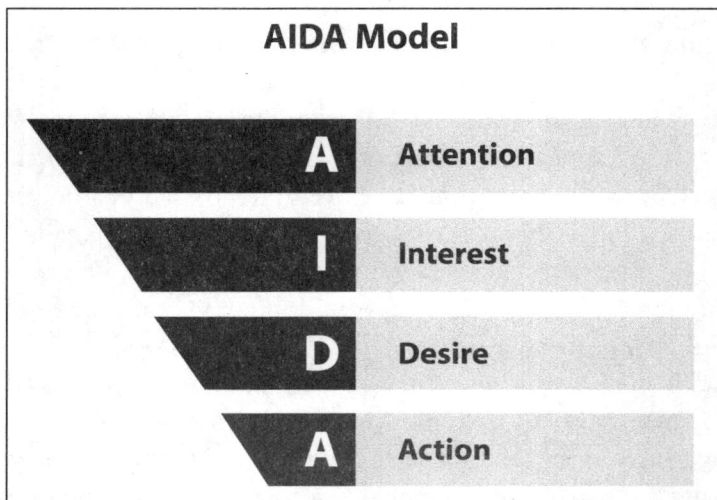

AIDA Model

A	Attention
I	Interest
D	Desire
A	Action

- **The McKinsey model:** This consumer decision journey uses a loop model rather than the linear one of the conventional sales funnel. It focuses on the interactions of a client that influence both their initial purchase decisions and their post-purchase experience. It also places an emphasis on UX and the importance of value-adding content that addresses real-world problems.

McKinsey Model

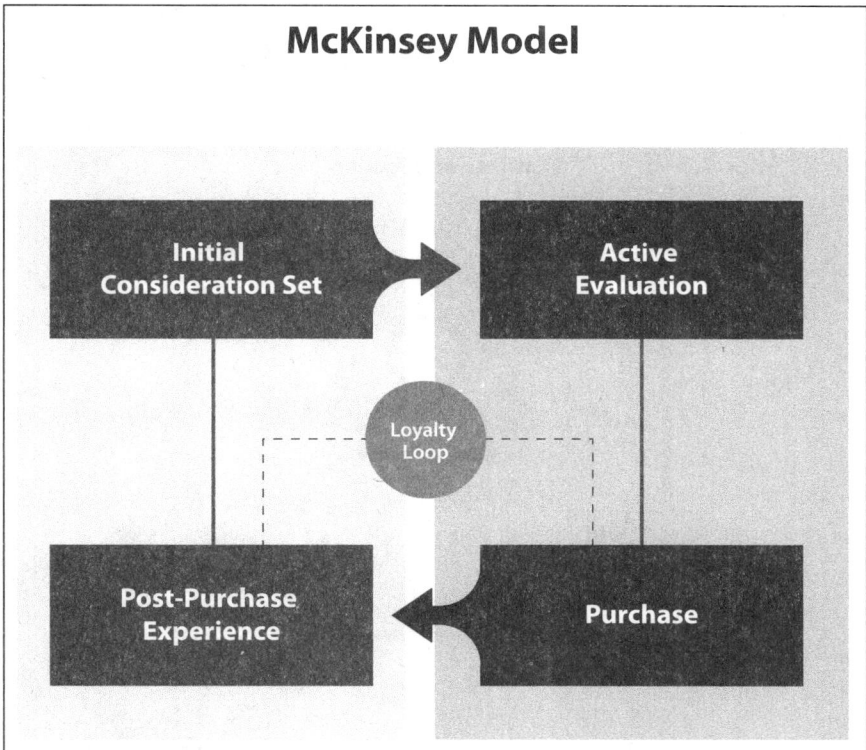

- **The Forrester model:** A client lifecycle model, this one puts the client at the center of a brand's marketing strategy. To this end, it recognizes marketing as a continuous effort and a holistic brand experience spanning four relationship phases: Discovery, Exploration, Purchase, and Engagement.

91

Forrester Model

Initial Purchase
Growth and Retention
Additional Purchases

ENGAGEMENT

DISCOVERY

PURCHASE

EXPLORATION

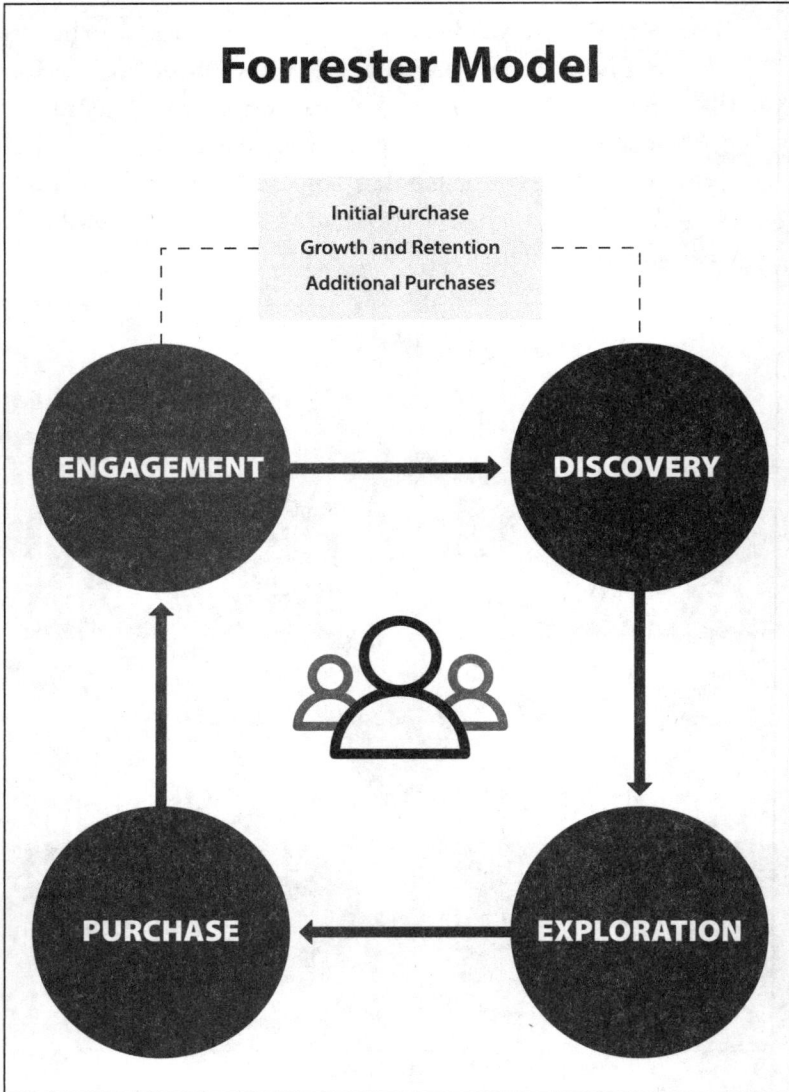

- **The RACE model:** An acronym for reach, act, convert, and engage, this model focuses on how sales and marketing teams nurture buyers and buying groups throughout each stage of the sales funnel. Each phase represents a desired goal with the end goal being to turn prospects beyond clients to become brand advocates.

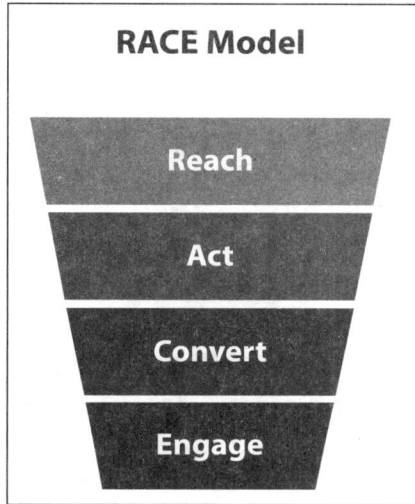

RACE Model

Reach

Act

Convert

Engage

- **The HubSpot flywheel:** Designed to closely align with the B2B purchase process in today's predominantly service-based economy, the flywheel envisages a continuous stream of leads. Consisting of multiple layers, it places growth in the center, with attraction, delight, and engagement on an inner ring and the people involved in the purchase process on an outer ring.

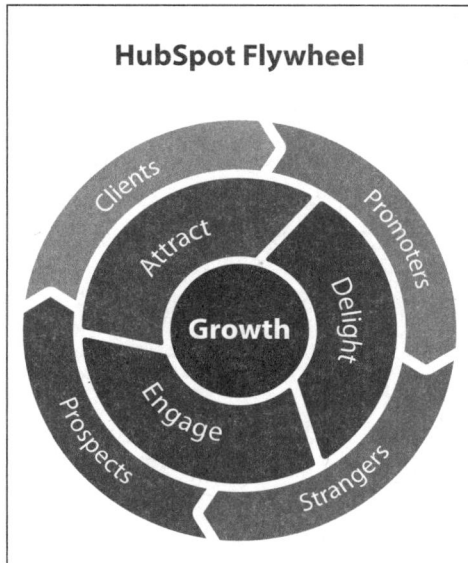

HubSpot Flywheel

Clients

Promoters

Attract

Delight

Growth

Prospects

Engage

Strangers

The sales funnel remains a marketing staple for good reason, but it's hugely beneficial to explore alternative strategies that are a better fit for your buyer journey to not become limited by its structure. However, rather than ditching the sales funnel entirely, your team should challenge and fine-tune it, as well as combine it with other methods to gain a better view into the behavior of your buyers and buying groups.

#91 AVOID FOCUSING ONLY ON BOTTOM-OF-FUNNEL PROSPECTS

Focusing on the bottom of the funnel is the obvious choice when it comes to nurturing and securing sales opportunities. After all, they are buyers who have been assessed according to your MQL criteria, and their lead score indicates they're ready to become SQLs.

However, this is a limiting strategy. A 2022 study by LinkedIn's B2B Institute found that only 5 percent of a company's total addressable market (TAM) genuinely has intent to buy. Focusing on BOFU can result in up to 95 percent of your potential buyers and their buying groups being overlooked. Most of these buyers may already be in your sales funnel at the TOFU or MOFU stages, and with the right nurturing strategy, you can mitigate the risks of them dropping out.

You must approach nurturing as a full-funnel strategy to also appeal to the broader audience who are "not in-market." These include prospective buyers who are not actively seeking or showing interest in a product or service at a given time. However, just because they're not in the buying phase of the buyer's journey doesn't mean they can't be nurtured over time to become potential clients.

Imagine, for example, a B2B SaaS company that provides tools for remote work. An in-market prospect might have recently transitioned to a remote work model and be actively looking for tools that will help their teams collaborate. Now, consider another company with a strong culture of in-office work that hasn't considered remote work as a viable alternative due to technical constraints. They might not be in-market now, but if they start to see the value in having tools that facilitate remote collaboration, there's a good chance they'll move into the in-market phase soon. With the right strategy in place, your nurturing content could be what convinces them of the virtues of remote or hybrid work.

#92 INVEST IN CLIENT RELATIONSHIP MANAGEMENT SOLUTIONS

Many brands use more than one sales funnel tool to orchestrate the buyer's journey and track interactions with their buyers. Long the industry standard, client relationship management suites (CRMs) are perhaps the most important software in any marketing team's tech stack. Many smaller companies use a single CRM that supports all major marketing channels, as well as landing pages, emails, and social media.

Modern CRM solutions are heavily integrated and data driven. They're usually web based and are updated regularly to support new marketing processes and sales models. CRMs also offer a range of automation tools to facilitate and scale outreach. The automation available via CRMs helps with many routine marketing processes, including email campaigns, social media publishing, and instant messaging.

Heatmap tools offer another powerful way to identify touchpoints that you might not even know exist, as well as where visitors disengage with your website. They're one of the best sales funnel analysis solutions, since they provide you with a much better understanding of user experiences. A heatmap detects how and where visitors interact both the most and least with your website, while also giving you an idea of where they enter the sales funnel and where they bounce back to the search engine results pages (SERPs).

For example, if visitors often interact with a specific case study or white paper, marketers can emphasize the particular use case or product features it showcases in their follow-up emails and other targeted content. Insights gathered from heatmaps can also be used to build highly effective landing pages that can be further optimized with A/B testing to see what performs best.

#93 EXPAND YOUR OMNICHANNEL MARKETING APPROACH

The goal of omnichannel marketing is to create a seamless experience across multiple online and, potentially, offline channels. It's a client-centric approach to the buying journey that puts the buyer at the center of the strategy, rather than focusing purely on business needs. It expands upon cross and multichannel marketing to emphasize the need for interactivity to drive engagement.

By expanding and aligning your omnichannel marketing efforts with each phase of the buying journey in mind, you can ensure your communications aren't just consistent, but also relevant, timely, and delivered through the most appropriate channels.

For example, a prospect at the top of the funnel might first learn about your brand from a post on LinkedIn. Then, if they like what they see, they may visit your website and read your blog posts, moving down the funnel in the process. Eventually, they might be sufficiently compelled to exchange their contact details on a lead capture page to download a white paper. At that point, they've moved to the middle of the funnel and could be qualified as an MQL. In this example, they've interacted with three distinct channels: LinkedIn, your business blog, and gated content via a lead capture page.

This is of course a relatively simplistic example. In practice, B2B buyers require nurturing over several months or even a year or more. During that time, they might attend events such as webinars or keynotes, sign up to your email newsletters, or both. You need to give them all the engagement options they're likely to use, so that they can shape their buyer's journey to their unique preferences, hence the importance of omnichannel marketing.

#94 DON'T DRIVE TOO QUICKLY FOR A CONVERSION

Of course, the overarching goal of any sales and marketing strategy is to move prospective buyers through their buying journey to the point they convert into clients. The primary obstacle with this in B2B purchases is the heavy dependence on a strong understanding of your target audience, as well as on how much rapport you've built with your prospects. If you're only looking at the end goal (i.e., driving conversions), chances are you'll lose sight of the importance of everything that comes in between.

While it can take months for prospective buyers to progress from leads to MQLs and then SQLs, that's not necessarily a problem. After all, if you offer an expensive and complex solution that takes months for clients to implement even in the best-case scenario, you can hardly expect buyers to make a purchase decision in your favor quickly.

We talked about the importance of having a full-funnel strategy earlier, but patience is also a strategic imperative. As the saying goes, it's not about the destination; it's about the journey, and in the case of B2B purchases, each stage of that journey plays a crucial role in guiding buyers and buying groups toward a decision.

Rushing prospects too quickly through the process without adequately addressing their concerns and needs along the way will only lead to mistrust. Even if it does still lead to a sale, client satisfaction might be at risk (and they might even churn). It's akin to skipping chapters in a novel: no matter how well written the story is, the ending won't make sense, because the context has been lost.

We'll delve deeper into nurturing through relationship building in chapter 8, but it's a vital element of optimizing the sales funnel to avoid putting all the focus on conversions and, instead, prioritize relationships.

#95 AUDIT AND ENHANCE YOUR DATA SOURCES AND CONTACT LISTS

Data is the backbone of any optimized sales funnel, and it should inform every decision your team makes. However, data is only as useful as its accuracy and relevance. If it's outdated or misaligned with your current business priorities, data can do more harm than good. Regularly auditing and enriching your data sources and contact lists isn't just best practice: it's a necessity.

Your CRM and other databases, including your contact lists, need to be routinely cleansed of outdated and incorrect data, either of which can lead to wasted resources and missed opportunities. For example, if you're targeting a buying group based on old information, you might end up addressing irrelevant pain points in your messaging.

Next, enrich your cleansed client data with intent data. Demographic, technographic, and firmographic data provide a valuable snapshot of your buyers, buying groups, and accounts, but combining it with intent data gives you a more dynamic view of their current needs and interests. For instance, if a company recently expanded its team, that might indicate a potential need for new software licenses or training services.

Automated tools have become a practical necessity for auditing and enhancing today's often massive datasets and contact lists. Data validation tools can automatically flag things like duplicate entries and incorrect or outdated data. These typically use a combination of AI, machine learning, and cross-referencing of data sources to draw attention to discrepancies that highlight areas in need of attention.

#96   STAY CLEAR OF UNPRODUCTIVE PURSUITS

Keeping your datasets fresh also helps ensure that you don't end up chasing lost causes. These include prospects who have already found a solution or whose circumstances have changed. For example, there's no point in targeting a buyer who's recently decided to opt for a competing product, unless pivoting to a long-term competitive displacement strategy happens to be a viable option.

While this might be obvious, it's often tempting to continue engaging buyers who would otherwise fit your ideal client profile (ICP). However, there's still value in knowing who these prospects are and why they fell out of the consideration. In some cases, their dropping out might be due to factors entirely beyond your control, but they can still inform the negative buyer personas that we talked about in chapter 1.

In other cases, a failure to convert might be entirely due to a problem on your end. Examples include a lack of coherent and relevant marketing collateral, slow response times, or perhaps an issue with the product itself. In certain situations, you may be able to reengage these buyers, but there is no guarantee. It's important to understand when to pivot to avoid wasting time with buyers and buying groups who are no longer interested.

Remember, every company has limited resources, time perhaps being the scarcest. For every minute you spend trying to follow an unproductive pursuit, you risk losing an opportunity to follow up with one who's a better fit for your business.

#97 STRIVE TO DECREASE COMPLEXITY IN YOUR BUYING PROCESS

Buyers are not only facing increasingly complex buying decisions but are also under mounting pressure to drive operational efficiency. Outreach that enables buyers to quickly identify and understand pain points, while empowering them to take action, becomes key to earning the favor of decision-makers.

Some key topics to be discussed in outreach, content, and sales interactions are known industry problems, pain points informed by AI-driven prospect data analysis, and the latest updates in their specific industries and niches. These topics are essential for demonstrating a keen understanding of buyer needs.

As buyers focus on growth through streamlined approaches and efficiency, aligning with these priorities is crucial to earning the trust of buyers as they evolve to demand increased value and expertise from vendors.

#98 FOCUS ON BUILDING RELATIONSHIPS TO DRIVE CLTV

Longer sales cycles and defensive buyers have directly impacted client acquisition costs (CAC), adding to the importance of client retention. Establishing long-term relationships with a loyal client base is a surefire strategy for ensuring a reliable revenue flow, capable of bolstering an organization's operations even amid large-scale economic fluctuations.

As buyers seek to optimize operational efficiency and continue streamlining their tech stacks, SaaS companies, for example, face increased churn rates. Apart from the difficulties faced by this business model, this is also due to the rise of millennial and Gen Z buyers who are more likely to change vendors. Challenges such as these emphasize the importance of investing in client relationships to boost lifetime value.

Client Lifetime Value (CLTV) is a metric determining the total revenue a company can expect a single client to generate. To illustrate the impact of this metric on revenue, research has found that increasing retention by only 5 percent can lead to a boost in profits of more than 25 percent; and that existing clients spend 31 percent more than newly acquired buyers, making them prime targets for cross-selling and upselling initiatives.

Some tactics to foster long-term relationships with your clients are:

- Solid branding, bolstered by storytelling;
- Continued delivery of high-value content in post-sales nurturing;
- Client Success (CS) initiatives designed to help clients solve their challenges and achieve goals with your solution; and
- Engaging with and providing support to online communities.

#99 FOSTER BRAND EVANGELISM

Brand evangelists are loyal clients who voluntarily advocate for a brand or product in their communities. Serving as unbiased, third-party input on a brand's solutions, brand evangelists are a highly valuable asset that helps to attract new prospects and build trust, contributing to competitive positioning.

Referral programs, post-sales nurturing, and dedicated client success support can all contribute to fostering brand evangelism, which can then be leveraged in a series of different strategies to boost CLTV and acquisition. Brand evangelists can help with the production of social proof, as they are more likely to participate in case studies, testimonials, and industry events. Brand evangelists are also more likely to engage in social media communities and provide insightful feedback.

These are some of your most valuable clients, and as such must be recognized and celebrated as valued members of your communities. Featuring their success stories on your website, offering exclusive perks via loyalty and referral programs, and incorporating their feedback into product updates are some tactics you can leverage to ensure brand evangelists feel valued.

CHAPTER 8

CULTIVATING RELATIONSHIPS WITH NURTURING

$\mathbf{A}$s B2B markets evolve, so too do client needs and behavior. Your ability to nurture buyers and buying groups and cultivate lasting relationships depends on how well you can adapt to meet these changes. This is doubly true in highly competitive markets like SaaS.

B2B sales cycles are getting longer, having risen by over 30 percent for established enterprises and over 20 percent for startups in recent years. Furthermore, most prospective buyers aren't ready to buy due to common factors like existing budgetary or technical constraints, a lack of executive buy-in, or organization-wide knowledge gaps.

However, these buying groups might still be open to learning about your product, and they'll be happy if you're able to identify their pain points. They might not be ready to purchase just yet, and depending on the length of your typical sales cycle, they might not be for a while. Indeed, the long sales cycles of B2B purchases mean it's inherently difficult to prevent or even notice buyers and buying groups dropping out of the consideration. It's also harder to keep your content and outreach relevant over such long time spans.

Nurturing aims to mitigate these challenges. We know it works too, since nurtured leads produce an average 20 percent increase in sales opportunities compared to those who aren't nurtured. The businesses that do it best generate 50 percent more sales qualified leads at a 33 percent lower cost as well. In this chapter, we'll look at the best practices for building an effective nurturing campaign.

#100 REFOCUS YOUR STRATEGY ON BUILDING RELATIONSHIPS

It's often said that you're not selling products; you're selling experiences. Those experiences encompass every interaction that your potential and existing clients have with your business and its solutions.

Relationships play a major role in these experiences, especially in B2B industries, where trust and authority are key drivers of both purchase decisions and client retention. Building such relationships demands a significant investment in time and money, especially at scale, so it's essential to use the right sales model.

A client-centric nurturing strategy must focus on building relationships. To understand how this works, we need to start thinking about the relationship funnel. The relationship funnel is similar in structure to the AIDA sales funnel, with the key difference being that it puts the focus on the client's relationship with your brand.

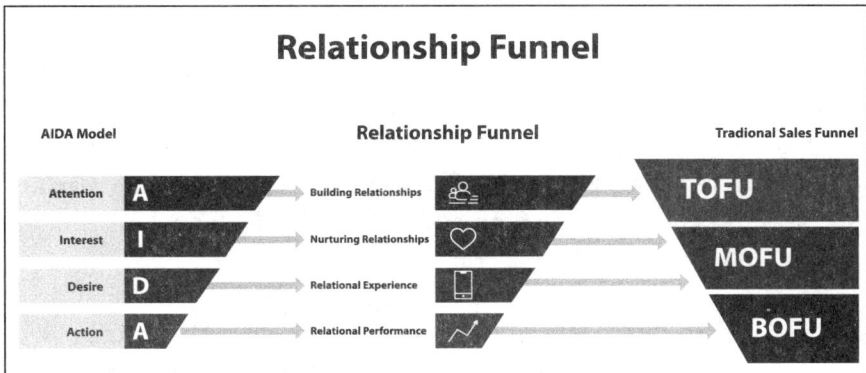

Relationship Funnel

AIDA Model		Relationship Funnel		Tradional Sales Funnel
Attention	A	Building Relationships		TOFU
Interest	I	Nurturing Relationships		MOFU
Desire	D	Relational Experience		BOFU
Action	A	Relational Performance		

1. **Attention:** In the relationship funnel, attention aligns with building relationships through strategies like demand generation.
2. **Interest:** Once you've piqued your target audience's interest, it's time to nurture those relationships with targeted content.

103

3. **Desire:** When a prospective buyer shows a desire to learn more about your solutions, you'll want to focus on their relational experience with your brand.
4. **Action:** Once they convert, it's time to focus on the performance of their relationship with your brand.

The relationship funnel is a great alternative to the sales funnel in B2B marketing, since it's better suited to longer sales cycles. It also features its own KPIs, the most important of which are the number of account renewals, up-sells and cross-sells, client acquisition costs (CAC), client lifetime value (CLTV), and return on relationship (ROR). ROR is the most direct measure of success in the relationship funnel, since it encompasses the total value a business receives from nurturing relationships with their buyers and buying groups.

#101 TELL A COMPELLING STORY WITH HUMAN-TO-HUMAN MARKETING

B2B decisions, while often seen as purely logical, still carry an emotional undertone. Even in buying groups, emotions like trust and confidence play a vital role in purchase decisions. Indeed, emotionally connected clients have a CLTV four times higher on average and are also more likely to recommend the brand. That's where human-to-human (H2H) marketing comes in:

- **Tell engaging stories:** The business world is sometimes criticized for its excessive use of jargon. Be sure to use relatable language used by prospects in your content to make it memorable and showcase the brand's human side.
- **Offer value-driven content:** Address genuine pain points without always pushing for a sale. This approach, especially earlier on in the funnel, fosters trust and showcases brand empathy.
- **Engage in online communities:** Brands that actively and helpfully participate in forums, without overtly promoting

their products, are seen as more authentic. For instance, a brand leader offering valuable advice on a platform can significantly boost brand perception.

- **Personalize email outreach:** While one-to-one emails are resource-intensive, tailoring emails to address specific pain points make interactions more human. Keep the tone professional yet approachable, keeping the prospect's needs at the forefront of messaging and emphasizing the human element behind the brand.

H2H marketing is all the more important in an era dominated by algorithms, data, and artificial intelligence. While automation is vital for scaling nurturing, there will always be cases that demand an authentic human touch. In fact, the best approach is to view automation as a way to free up time to do exactly that.

#102 ENRICH YOUR NURTURING CADENCES WITH DEMAND INTELLIGENCE

Demand intelligence is a combination of data points, according to your organization's unique goals and processes, collected by marketing and sales teams to bolster demand strategies. These data points often consist of segmentation details, buyer persona and ICP data, as well as performance data from former campaigns and any other relevant historical data.

Demand intelligence helps nurturing efforts, as well as other marketing initiatives, achieve high relevance and resonance with the target audience. First- and third-party data alike can be compiled into a single repository to build a powerful demand intelligence database, combining website analytics, CRM, email, and social media metrics, survey results, and intent and segmentation data, as well as industry trends and reports.

AI data analysis tools are powerful assets to identify hidden patterns in this data, gleaning valuable insights into your audience's needs, preferences, and behavior, accurately mapping buyer journeys and enabling nurturing campaigns to target buyers with great accuracy. This helps fuel the development of highly personalized, seamless buying experiences.

Initial efforts to structure demand intelligence will likely encounter gaps and blind spots in the data. Regardless, focus on working with what you have: forming and testing hypotheses across campaigns to authenticate, challenge, and refine your data.

#103 DIVERSIFY YOUR NURTURING STRATEGIES AND CHANNELS

The lengthy nature of buyer journeys and the importance of fostering long-term relationships with B2B buyers make diversifying nurturing strategies and channels imperative.

Although email nurturing has long been the industry standard, this strategy performs best when paired with other outreach methods, going beyond the inbox to reach users where they are. Not only does this tackle channel fatigue, but it also helps to promote a seamless buying experience across entire buying groups by appealing to a broader set of preferences.

Social media, for example, is a prime channel for delivering resonant nurturing, be it via regular publications, newsletters, inMail outreach, or paid advertising. After all, three in four B2B buyers report relying on social media to inform purchase decisions, and learning about new products and brands is one of the top motivations for using LinkedIn, alongside networking with peers and forging new connections.

Other strategies, such as targeted display ads and dynamic retargeting, can promote content according to specific buyer interests, allowing for the sharing of content that quickly addresses evolving pain points, which contributes to your brand's positioning. However, when utilizing paid advertising initiatives, it is crucial to support them with your latest demand intelligence, ensuring the best possible performance and, consequently, the highest ROI.

Finally, diversifying nurture channels and touchpoints enables your campaigns to earn insightful data on buyer behavior, shedding light on sources of friction and highlighting your most efficient tactics. Not only does this earn you valuable data to inform future campaigns, it also enables you to action on-flight optimizations to drive performance.

#104 BOOST ENGAGEMENT WITH NEXT-GENERATION CHATBOTS

Modern chatbots have emerged as an effective way to enhance and scale user engagement while placing visitors on nurturing tracks. Although some marketers remain skeptical, with concerns that chatbots can come off as impersonal, there's a big difference between the pre-scripted chatbots of old and the AI-powered ones available today.

Newer chatbots use the latest tech, such as natural language processing (NLP) and adaptive learning, to engage users in a more humanlike way. That certainly doesn't mean they can replace real sales or client service reps, but they're perfectly capable of answering a myriad of routine questions in short order.

When properly utilized, chatbots serve as an entry point into the buying journey by cutting down bounce rates and converting first-time visitors into prospective buyers. Best of all, every interaction is recorded, making attribution easier than ever. They can serve several purposes, among the most popular being to answer FAQs or to encourage prospects to subscribe to an email newsletter, download resources, or even sign up for a free trial.

Imagine, for example, a potential buyer visits your website and expresses an interest in one of your solutions. A chatbot can engage immediately, offering additional information and resources relevant to the user's interest. Moreover, by integrating a chatbot with your CRM, you can capture and analyze interactions at scale using tools like sentiment analysis. This expedites the optimization process, allowing you to better tailor your subsequent outreach efforts to the specific needs of your target audience.

#105 CREATE MULTIPLE NURTURING CADENCES WITH MANY TOUCHPOINTS

Relying solely on a one-size-fits-all approach to nurturing often falls short. Different buyers have distinct needs, preferences, and timelines. Moreover, those parameters can change with the times, hence the need for agility.

By creating multiple nurturing cadences with many touchpoints that span a range of channels, you can better cater to these varied requirements and increase the likelihood of a conversion. Here are some ways to achieve this:

- **Email:** Not every buyer is at the same stage in their journey, hence why segmenting your mailing list based on where they are in their buying process is essential. A new buyer may benefit from an onboarding series introducing your brand and its solutions, for example, while a more engaged prospect might appreciate a deep dive into specific product features.
- **Social:** Social networks are incredibly varied with unique features on each, which is why there's absolutely no point in using the same strategy for all of them. For example, X is better suited to a high volume of shorter posts, while LinkedIn prioritizes businesslike posts, focusing on thought leadership rather than quick news updates.
- **Events:** Whether in person or remote, events provide a unique opportunity to engage prospective buyers on their terms. Popular formats include everything from in-person trade fairs and conventions to online webinars and keynotes. However, following up with attendees after the event is critical, so consider crafting dedicated nurturing cadences for them too.

Personalization is key, regardless of the channel. Ensure your content speaks directly to your buyers' pain points and interests while taking into account where they are in their buyer journey. Use data-driven insights to tailor your messages and regularly review and adjust your strategy by proactively monitoring the performance of your cadences.

#106 ADOPT PROVEN RETARGETING PRACTICES TO ENGAGE BUYERS WHO HAVE NOT CONVERTED YET

B2B buying groups are commonly composed of busy leadership members, so there's always a high risk of buyers going cold. On the other hand, the last thing you want to do is waste resources on bombarding them with marketing content they're not interested in, alienating them through the process.

Strategic retargeting is vital, simply because only 2 percent of web traffic converts at a first visit. But that doesn't mean the other 98 percent should be neglected. Chances are that many of those 98 percent have either forgotten about your brand or require further convincing that you can offer the solutions they're looking for.

Once again, personalization is vital. Creating the right nurturing cadences helps to avoid brand blindness and aggravation. Throughout each cadence, your messaging must be tailored to suit your buyers' behavior. Timing and frequency are equally important, since no one wants to receive a slew of sales emails over a short period. Thus, B2B retargeting takes time, necessitating a thoughtful approach that respects your buyers' unique challenges and pain points, as well as where they are in the buyer journey.

Avoid overusing the same retargeting ads or messaging, even if they're working with the target audience. Just because they're performing well at a given time doesn't mean they will continue to do so as conditions change. Continuous improvement and adaptation are paramount, hence the power of A/B testing whenever you're crafting new retargeting collateral.

#107 LEVERAGE GAMIFICATION TO INCREASE ENGAGEMENT

Gamification is one of the biggest movements in marketing and user experience and, contrary to popular belief, is not only relevant in B2C. In fact, B2B organizations should consider the successes B2C companies have had with gamification and explore ways to incorporate it into their own nurturing strategies.

Many B2B companies, especially those in the software industry, now use gamification, which broadly refers to the use of tactics normally associated with games to keep people engaged. Common strategies include boosting engagement with interactive quizzes or games that educate potential clients with simulations, or foster a sense of community and competition with leaderboards and reward systems.

Gamification works because it taps into our inherent psychology. For busy businesspeople, there are few things more satisfying than crossing an item off their to-do list, especially when they receive recognition for doing so. For example, completing a task in Asana, the popular project management tool, makes one of five "celebration creatures" occasionally appear on the screen.

It might sound like a gimmick, especially in the typically formal world of B2B, but there's no denying that incorporating fun elements gives audiences a much-needed dopamine hit. In nurturing, adding that dash of magic to a sales pitch can make you more memorable by delivering a fun and unique experience. It's especially effective in interactive demos or for onboarding prospects in free trials.

#108 TAKE A METHODICAL APPROACH IN YOUR FOLLOW-UP EFFORTS

Timing is everything in marketing communications, and nurturing is no exception. Even the most compelling content will fall on deaf ears if it's sent at the wrong time, both in terms of the time of day or week and where your buyers find themselves in their buyer journeys.

In fact, it's more important to reach out to buyers and buying groups when you know they have a specific and timely need.

While there are few hard-and-fast rules on exactly when to follow up, the industry standard is a good starting point. For example, you should generally follow up with new leads within an hour of receiving their contact information, since they'll most likely remember that interaction. However, it is still important to consider the time of day. For example, if a prospect gives you their contact information after the end of their working day, it is much better to follow up the next morning.

Naturally, it makes sense to follow up with prospects during regular business hours, with the possible exception of Fridays. If you serve multiple time zones, you should also take that into account when setting up automated follow-ups. If there's a genuine need, it typically takes five to eight follow-up emails before you should consider a buyer unresponsive, depending on the length of your sales cycle.

Frequency is perhaps even more important than timing, and it's one of the hardest to get right. Following up too often during a short period will risk annoying recipients. Wait too long, and there's a high chance they'll forget about you. The optimal frequency depends on the length of your sales cycle, but a good rule of thumb is to send the second follow-up a week later, the third a month later, and any subsequent follow-up every three months thereafter. However, you should always optimize your follow-up strategy based on the data you collect during the process.

#109 BUILD TRUST THROUGH OPEN CONVERSATIONS

Nurturing should always be conversational. Focus on developing relationships instead of closing deals, especially during the top and middle stages of the sales funnel. Remember, the goal is to build and maintain trust and, in doing so, offer progressively greater value to your prospective clients. That means positioning yourself as an industry expert and trusted solution provider.

Before you develop nurturing content, speak with your existing clients. Book meetings with your most loyal clients, conduct surveys, and comment on their LinkedIn posts. Better yet, ask your best clients if they'd be willing to have you interview them for a case study. Not only are case studies extremely valuable for nurturing buyers and buying groups, the interviews they're based on also give you firsthand insights into your client's experience.

There are also indirect, yet still highly effective, ways to nurture buyers. There's a good chance that they will be reading reviews about your business on G2 and similar platforms. Taking the time to respond to these reviews, particularly the less-than-favorable ones, is an effective way to mitigate objections and demonstrate transparency. The importance of active listening cannot be overstated.

Some B2B marketers have even gone so far as to adopt a radical transparency approach. By providing clear insights into processes, pricing, challenges, and even admitting to limitations, you can foster deep connections with your buyers. While admittedly controversial, radical transparency stands out as a genuine commitment to client centricity, especially at a time when clients are increasingly skeptical of marketing tactics.

#110 DEVELOP STRATEGIES AND ASSETS TO OVERCOME OBSTACLES

Effective nurturing requires you to anticipate and address obstacles and objections head-on. This requires a deep understanding of potential clients' challenges, in response to which you'll create tailored content that speaks directly to these concerns. Remember, hesitation is almost a given in the competitive B2B landscape, even more so if you offer a high-value product with a lengthy sales cycle.

Your messaging should consistently position your brand as an industry expert. You're not just a company selling a product, but a trustworthy advisor. You need to demonstrate how you've successfully overcome the same challenges that your potential clients are navigating now. Whether you're reaching out via email campaigns, LinkedIn messages, or cold calls, it's vital to communicate with authenticity and show genuine interest in the needs of your target audience.

When crafting content, don't just provide generic solutions with the goal of generating as much traffic as possible. Instead, craft content that solves the precise problems your target audience is facing to drive qualified interest in your brand.

For example, if a potential client is grappling with excess inventory, offer more than a basic guide on inventory management. Instead, delve into detailed strategies like deploying a just-in-time inventory system, leveraging flash sales, and exploring partnerships for bundled product promotions. Highlighting real-world examples demonstrates your areas of expertise and helps you to establish relationships built on trust and authenticity.

Finally, keep in mind that B2B buyers usually share the content you produce with their buying groups, if it offers enough value, so make sure it stands as a testament to your brand's quality.

#111 NURTURE YOUR CLIENTS, EVEN AFTER YOU GET A SALE

In B2B, nurturing doesn't conclude with a sale. In fact, post-sale nurturing is essential to fostering long-term loyalty and maximizing CLTV. On the other hand, when clients are treated merely as transactions, client satisfaction will inevitably suffer, and churn will increase. Nurturing must transition seamlessly into long-term client relationship management. It's a team effort that should last for the entirety of a client's experience with your business.

Your newest clients should get value out of your solutions as soon as possible. The sooner they do, the sooner they'll become loyal brand advocates who are more likely to refer your business to their peers. This, in turn, can reduce future sales cycles.

To make this happen, be sure to prioritize onboarding. Provide dedicated support, training sessions, and resource guides to help them get the most out of your product or service. For example, a SaaS vendor might offer in-app tutorials to guide new clients through the platform's key functions.

Staying present with regular communication is just as important. Reach out to clients to ask how their experience is going and if there's anything you can do to help them. Content drips, such as email newsletters and personalized emails, are ideal for sharing insights and industry news, as well as relevant updates about your own offerings. For instance, if you've launched a new feature update or published a white paper specific to your client's industry, be sure to share it with them. By continuously adding value through a combination of onboarding and personalized content, you're more likely to upsell and cross-sell additional services too.

#112 SPEED UP YOUR SALES CYCLES WITH AUTOMATION SOFTWARE

Marketing automation tools help you scale demand generation and nurturing campaigns in a way that simply isn't possible if you're relying on manual means alone. With automation, you can free up time for marketers to focus on strategic initiatives and content development, as well as for sales reps to focus on building H2H relationships. Since every interaction is trackable, automation also ensures you don't end up losing sight of your buyers and buying groups.

Modern marketing automation software uses sophisticated processes to track buyer interaction, discern their stage in their sales cycle, and deliver the right content at the right time. It will also help you continuously improve your understanding of your target audience and develop stronger client profiles. For example, by closely monitoring how buyers and buying groups interact with your content, you can segment them into specific lists based on factors like pain points, industry niche, and the stage they're at in their buying journeys. Automation can grade them based on their interactions as well, so you can easily tell which ones are merely interested and which ones are genuinely considering a purchase.

A standout benefit of automated nurturing is its efficiency. No longer do sales teams have to spend significant time reaching out to cold prospects. Instead, the automated nurturing process helps move them down the funnel to the point it's truly worthwhile for a sales rep to engage them directly. Moreover, automation helps identify any bottlenecks in the funnel. For instance, if a large number of prospective buyers drop off after receiving a particular email, it might be time to evaluate the content or timing of that email.

Drip email campaigns are another prime opportunity for automation. Drip emails are triggered by specific actions, such as a prospect leaving their contact info to download a gated white paper or signing up for a product demo. Just ensure you tailor the email content to the relevant actions and buying journey stage and establish the optimal timing. You can automate much of the rest.

#113 COMMUNICATE CONSISTENTLY ACROSS ALL MARKETING CHANNELS

In the highly competitive world of B2B marketing, consistency is the beacon that guides buyers to where you want them to be. While each channel has its unique nuances, and each buyer has a distinctive journey, your brand must resonate uniformly across all cadences and their respective touchpoints. This consistency not only helps people remember you; it also builds trust and ensures that buyers and buying groups always know what to expect from your brand, regardless of how and where they interact with it.

Consistent communication serves as the foundation for any strong brand image. When buyers encounter the same tone, messaging, and visual elements across different channels, it helps reinforce their understanding of your brand and, by extension, your solutions. This uniformity ensures that, even as buyers move through the various stages of the buying journey, the core messaging remains the same.

As we mentioned earlier in this guide, it can help enormously to have guidelines in the form of a brand book. This shouldn't be taken as a rigid set of rules, but rather as a way to encourage collaboration and uniformity between business departments. After all, your messaging must be personalized but consistent.

Let's take a SaaS company as an example. For their more technical audience personas, they might emphasize the technical aspects of their product on a platform like GitHub, but focus on its user-friendly interface on LinkedIn or X. The central theme remains the same, as do the tone, voice, and other branding elements.

CHAPTER 9

ALIGNING TEAMS FOR REVENUE OPERATIONS SUCCESS

In larger organizations, it is common for sales, marketing, and client success teams to be siloed, which creates challenges for data sharing and collaboration. Each department also often has their own strategies and priorities, which can lead to teams pursuing different departmental goals, rather than what is beneficial for the business as a whole.

According to HubSpot, 57 percent of sales and marketing budgets go toward client acquisition. Yet retaining clients and maximizing CLTV is at least as important. As HubSpot describes it, business growth is no longer a funnel, but a flywheel consisting of acquiring, engaging, and delighting clients to the point they restart the cycle. But like every wheel, friction exists at each contact point. Examples include poor tooling, a lack of internal collaboration, and siloed data, as previously discussed.

Fortunately, times are changing. Enter RevOps, also known as revenue operations, a strategy for tackling the challenges of fragmented revenue-generating functions head on. The ultimate goal of RevOps is to unify sales, marketing, client success, and other departments' functions to ensure a streamlined process driven by aligned goals and a cohesive strategy focused on growth and the overall buyer's journey.

In previous chapters, we looked at ways to connect with clients during each stage of the buyer journey. Now we're going to explore how to get your teams aligned to make that possible.

#114 UNDERSTAND THE LINK BETWEEN REVOPS AND CLIENT EXPERIENCE

RevOps and client experience are inextricably intertwined. Client experience is everything a brand does to deliver the most value to clients, while RevOps refers to the internal strategy and processes that make that possible, all while driving revenue.

At its core, RevOps seeks to optimize the entire client journey from the first touchpoint to post-sale interactions. The alignment of sales, marketing, and client success teams is what facilitates this process.

One way to view the connection between RevOps and client experience is with the concept of the flywheel, an alternative to the traditional sales funnel popularized by HubSpot. RevOps plays a central role in the flywheel model by addressing the forces and friction at each stage of the buyer's journey.

Force refers to strategies that accelerate the flywheel, thereby enhancing client experiences and speeding up sales cycles. Friction, on the other hand, refers to the obstacles clients and prospects face during their journey, as well as any internal challenges that prevent you from serving them effectively.

Lengthy response times, difficulties navigating a website, or confusion over pricing plans are all common sources of friction. These particular examples all start from within the organization as well, hence the importance of addressing internal processes first. One of the most common challenges is the widespread lack of alignment between internal teams which, in turn, can lead to higher employee turnover, poor collaboration, and even a problematic business culture.

RevOps is all about alignment in pursuit of a seamless client experience. It's akin to tidying up your home before welcoming guests. With a synchronized effort to provide the best possible client experience, you can foster loyalty and drive sustainable growth.

#115 IMPLEMENT CX-FOCUSED STRATEGIES AIDED BY GREAT UX DESIGN

High-quality client experiences (CX) are one of the main drivers of RevOps models and have the potential to drive long-term brand loyalty, supporting renewals and expansion opportunities. CX's impact on revenue is often championed by Client Success teams, dedicated to ensuring a high-quality experience that caters to each client's unique needs and preferences.

Locating and removing sources of friction, both in the buyer's journey and internal processes, is the key motion to improving the client experience, by promoting a seamless, user-friendly, and engaging product/service. Internally, optimizing inefficient or unnecessary processes and implementing a single source of truth to avoid data silos are key tactics to reduce friction.

Externally, however, a focus on equipping your products and channels, such as your website, with high-quality UX (user experience) is one of the most important courses of action to promote frictionless CX. Poorly structured websites that make it difficult for users to locate the content they need, for example, may frustrate prospects and harm buyer enablement. Mandatory sales interaction for tasks that could operate on a self-serve basis, especially in an era of increasingly independent buyers, can also be aversive for prospects conducting research. Finally, long wait times for support requests or even a lack of response are points of friction that may discourage renewals and undermine relationship building.

#116 BREAK DOWN SILOS TO GAIN A HOLISTIC VIEW OF YOUR CLIENTS

Silos can be the Achilles' heel of any business. These silos, often formed due to departmental structures, differing goals, or disparate technology stacks, hinder a company's ability to view their clients holistically. When departments operate in isolation, they miss out on the broader context of client interactions, leading to disjointed client experiences and missed opportunities. RevOps seeks to solve these problems with a radical rethink of the traditional business structure.

Start by addressing the technological barriers. Focus on building a reduced, integrated, and optimized tech stack that streamlines data sharing between departments. Instead of piling on tools, rid yourself of the ones that don't work well with your main platforms, and focus on solutions that prioritize integration.

The goal is to centralize your data to have a single source of truth (SSoT). An integrated data platform not only ensures data accuracy but also facilitates the merging of insights from automation, enablement, and product data. The result is that all stakeholders, from sales to marketing to client success, gain a comprehensive view of the client's journey, including their preferences and pain points. This facilitates pivots and optimization.

Once you have your tech stack in order, you can start focusing on the human element. Better tech itself helps drive a culture of collaboration and accountability, but you must not overlook the importance of strong leadership. Encourage a business culture where each revenue-facing team sees themselves as part of a larger ecosystem, all working toward the same overarching goal of enhancing the client experience.

#117 DEFINE YOUR ROLES, RESPONSIBILITIES, AND PROCESSES CLEARLY

RevOps depends on a clear definition of roles, responsibilities, and processes. This planning stage is vital for closing the gap between sales and marketing, optimizing business functions, and overcoming inefficiencies in revenue cycles.

Appoint a RevOps manager to oversee the entire strategy. Their job is to achieve and preserve alignment across sales, marketing, and client success, as well as continuously optimize revenue processes. Next, appoint a data analyst to oversee the metrics and analytics providing insight into strategies and trends. You'll also need a systems integrator responsible for ensuring your tech stack is optimized to function cohesively. Another key role is the process designer, whose job is to meticulously craft workflows and processes that eliminate inefficiencies during sales cycles. Some of these roles, such as data analysts and systems integrators, are commonly outsourced.

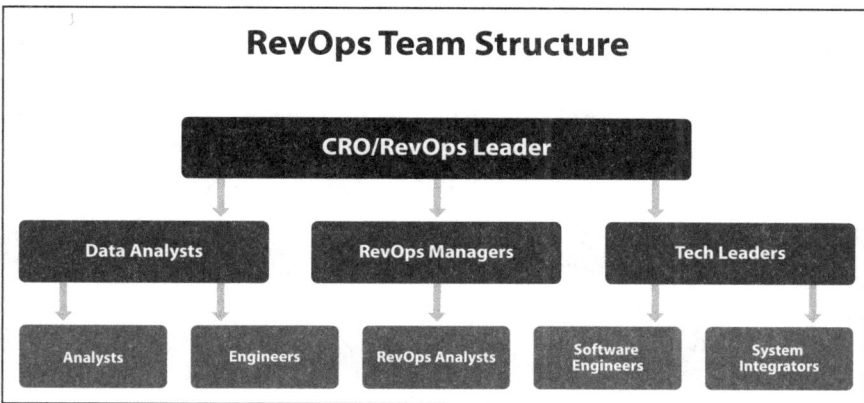

RevOps Team Structure

CRO/RevOps Leader

Data Analysts	RevOps Managers	Tech Leaders

Analysts	Engineers	RevOps Analysts	Software Engineers	System Integrators

RevOps teams must prioritize communication and transparency. This must start from the top, with the overarching goal being to foster an environment where everyone has the opportunity to contribute. Be sure to guide teams with company values, especially when onboarding new team members. This inclusive approach amplifies efficiency and bolsters team morale. When everyone feels heard and valued for their efforts, the collective output is often even greater than the sum of its parts.

#118 SHARE KNOWLEDGE OF BUYER PERSONAS FOR CLOSER ALIGNMENT

Sharing knowledge across teams is a fundamental goal of RevOps. In contrast, when teams operate in silos, they are likely to miss out on the collective wisdom and insights of their colleagues. This is especially true when understanding a company's client base. Buyer personas, for example, are commonly viewed as being relevant to sales and marketing teams, but they also have a role to play in any client-facing team.

By sharing knowledge of buyer personas across the board, teams like those involved in lead management, onboarding new clients, or client support will be better equipped to satisfy clients' desire for a smooth experience and hassle-free service. It also promotes consistency in messaging, thus strengthening your brand. That's a substantial improvement on fragmented environments where clients may feel that transitioning between sales and service are like working with two completely different companies.

To further promote a transparent environment, be sure to recognize and reward knowledge sharing. Positive reinforcement is highly effective, and it helps overcome the communication barriers between teams. When team members naturally feel the need to communicate with their coworkers, that's a clear sign of a productive workplace. Moreover, it gives teams access to new insights, recommendations, tips, and suggestions that they might not otherwise have considered. Finally, get company executives on board to lead by example, while also ensuring their own knowledge becomes embedded in company culture.

These factors combine to create a better working environment, and that leads to better client experiences. After all, a seamless buyer journey depends on having well-structured internal processes.

#119 HOLD REGULAR MEETINGS BETWEEN KEY STAKEHOLDERS

When it comes to running a productive business and minimizing friction in the buyer journey, there are multiple factors that can derail the process. Some examples include meetings starting late or running over, missing or late attendees, poorly captured notes, or a general lack of camaraderie. The unfortunate reality is that, while businesses spend around 15 percent of their time on meetings, 71 percent of them are considered unproductive.

While maintaining a culture of communication and engagement requires regular meetings, they should be rigidly scheduled and planned, ideally weekly. These can focus on wins, misses, and any questions concerning help needed. You'll also want to bring all full-time members of your RevOps team together for monthly and quarterly business reviews to keep everyone on the right track.

While scheduling and timing are vital from a practical point of view, it's just as important to ensure meetings are engaging and productive. Put your employees at the center stage by treating them as internal clients, rather than focusing entirely on wider business goals. By empowering team members to contribute to the conversation, you'll likely uncover insights and potential new strategies.

Whether it's a Teams call or an in-person roundtable, your RevOps meetings serve two main purposes: sharing knowledge and humanizing interdepartmental interaction. For example, instead of communicating through long email chains, virtual or in-person meetings help by putting faces to names. This approach also makes your business far more welcoming for new hires, especially in the era of remote and hybrid work, where it can be harder to foster and preserve company culture.

#120 DETERMINE WHICH KPIs AND ROI METRICS TO SHARE

RevOps metrics help businesses identify areas of improvement and measure their progress toward new goals. They're a vital part of any collaborative decision-making effort toward driving revenue. By contrast, in a siloed environment, each team may have their own way of tracking performance, which often doesn't align with those of other teams. For example, sales teams typically focus more on monthly revenue, while marketing teams might focus on metrics such as website traffic.

By sharing KPIs between departments, companies can foster a culture of accountability and transparency, thus leading to improved performance. Of course, the qualifiers for KPIs vary for each team, given their different roles and responsibilities. What's important is that they also have shared KPIs so that different teams aren't solely focused on their individual goals. Here are some examples:

- **Revenue growth:** Arguably the king of the balance sheet, revenue growth is a strategy as much as it is a goal. It's also the main reason why RevOps exists, so it's important to make it the number one metric for your team to strive for.
- **Revenue retention:** Bringing in revenue is one thing, but retaining it depends on many different factors, such as how satisfied clients are with your business and how efficient your sales and post-sales processes are.
- **Client acquisition costs:** Many factors influence how much it costs to acquire a new client, and they're not all related to sales and marketing expenses. For example, a great client experience can lead to referrals, thereby reducing CAC.
- **Sales pipeline velocity:** B2B sales cycles are generally much longer than in B2C. While this is unlikely to change, leveraging RevOps to facilitate a smooth buyer journey can significantly reduce sales cycle length.

Different teams will still have their own metrics to track, some of which might not be relevant to others. However, grouping them under the umbrella of shared KPIs (like those above) will help unite departments through common goals.

#121 COORDINATE YOUR CONTENT MARKETING CAMPAIGNS WITH SALES

The term "content marketing" is perhaps somewhat misleading. A robust content strategy goes beyond marketing to incorporate the entire buyer journey. However, many businesses still see content as little more than a way to generate search traffic or keep buyers engaged with email campaigns.

These are both important parts of any comprehensive content strategy. That said, your content should also span nurturing, sales, and post-sales support. That's why you should develop a company-wide content strategy by working closely across sales, marketing, and client experience. For example, marketing content includes everything from paid ad copy to email newsletters. By contrast, sales content encompasses formats like product comparisons, case studies, and personal testimonials. Content tailored for client success teams includes any assets that help existing clients or trial users get greater value out of your solutions.

Co-creating elements of the content strategy will help your teams align their understanding of buyer behavior, such as interests, goals, pain points, and roles in decision-making processes. Some individual pieces of content also span multiple stages of the buyer journey. For instance, the marketing team might use a webinar to raise awareness about a topic or solution, while the sales team might use it as a touchpoint to engage potential buyers by answering live questions during a call.

Many content formats can serve as a bridge between awareness, consideration, decision, and post-purchase stages. However, for any such content to be effective, it requires the unique insights and experiences of multiple teams to craft content that resonates. Even for content that serves a singular purpose, it's important that the broader RevOps board be informed of when each campaign goes live to facilitate a seamless transition from one touchpoint to the next.

#122 MAP OUT THE BUYER'S JOURNEY TO STREAMLINE THE SALES HANDOFF

Aligning teams requires a continuous analysis and documentation of the buyer's journey. This includes a deep dive into buyers' objectives, the touchpoints they engage with, their preferred communication channels, and the points at which they typically convert.

As buyer behavior evolves, teams must keep one another updated. Equipped with a mutual understanding, they can adapt their sales and marketing processes accordingly. For example, rather than focusing solely on new prospects, develop a nurturing program that prioritizes retention and repeat purchases. After all, it's often more cost-effective to retain existing clients than to acquire new ones.

With your buyer journeys accurately mapped out, you'll have a strong foundation in place for streamlining the transition from marketing to sales. Begin by clearly stating the characteristics that define a qualified lead or, as we talked about in chapter 7, what makes an MQL become an SQL. In B2B, buyers should exhibit clear intent to buy, as defined by the lead scoring system.

Larger enterprises often use internal service level agreements (SLAs) to streamline the handoff process and make the obligations of each team clear. An SLA sets the criteria for handling, scoring, and transitioning buyers through their buying journey. Formalizing the process in this way ensures consistency and replicability while instilling confidence in its value.

A successful process depends on sharing information. Sales teams require comprehensive details about the incoming leads, so they can personalize the experience and ensure a smooth transition from MQL to SQL. Feedback loops are a critical part of the process, with sales teams relaying feedback on quality to marketing. Establish a review process that involves high-level executives from both teams, to validate rejections and drive improvements.

#123 HIRE SEASONED EXPERTS WITH A CLEAR UNDERSTANDING OF REVOPS

As a relatively new concept, it's not always easy to hire for RevOps, especially if you're building a full team from scratch. Moreover, there's no industry standard career path in the space. Managers often come from a background spanning sales or marketing or even both.

Others might come from a client experience background and have little experience with sales and marketing, but that doesn't necessarily preclude them from being suitable for a role as an internal champion for RevOps. Example job titles for such a role are RevOps Manager or Chief Revenue Officer. However, given the increase in the popularity of RevOps, job titles are not always the best basis for identifying candidates.

Start by establishing clear goals for your future RevOps team. By understanding what you aim to achieve, you can map out the roles and skills you need to reach those objectives and identify any existing skill gaps in your organization. For example, if your key goal is to bridge the gap between sales and marketing, you're going to want someone with experience in both domains.

Prioritize candidates with a rich background in your industry, especially in the fields of change management and other areas similar to RevOps. Those with experience in other operations areas, such as FinOps (financial operations) or DevOps (developer operations) might also be good potential candidates. For example, consider a scenario where the integration of new software faces resistance from the sales department. An expert with a background in DevOps who also has change management skills should be suitably equipped to help navigate such challenges and ensure a smooth adoption. Ultimately, this should depend on the priority skill set you believe is necessary for your organization.

Beyond hard skills and experience, hiring teams should also consider attitudes and soft skills. RevOps team members, by definition, must be team players, and that means being adaptable, communicative, and having a genuine passion for learning. For instance, a team member with a penchant for testing new things might proactively explore new tools and strategies for bringing innovative solutions to the table.

Finally, retaining talent is just as important as hiring. Genuine RevOps skills and expertise are hard to come by, so retention strategies are essential. By fostering a positive team culture, aligning company mission and values, and offering continuous learning opportunities, you can make your company a far more compelling place for talent to stay.

PART FOUR

MEASURING SUCCESS AND OPTIMIZING PERFORMANCE

If there's one constant in the world of marketing, it's change. Technology drives new trends in purchase behaviors, and market shifts put pressure on every industry to evolve. That's why you should never rely on set-and-forget marketing campaigns.

In part 3, we shared ways to nurture your buyers and buying groups, and delight existing clients. But what works now might not work next week, next month, or next year. Change is inevitable, and it can sometimes come without warning.

In part 4, we'll explore the importance of leveraging the right data and key performance indicators (KPIs) to drive continuous improvement. We'll wrap up our journey with a look at the future of digital marketing and how to better prepare your team for the unknown challenges ahead.

CHAPTER 10

EVALUATING SUCCESS WITH KEY PERFORMANCE INDICATORS

Every marketing campaign has different goals, whether it's raising brand awareness, growing sales, or maximizing CLTV. As a result, each campaign also comes with its own resource requirements, whether it's people's time and expertise or finances from the marketing budget. And, when company resources are involved, stakeholders will naturally want to be sure they're being invested optimally.

The unfortunate reality is that companies waste about half of their digital budgets due to factors like a lack of targeting, strategy, and team alignment. However, you can't fix a problem if you don't know where it lies, and you can't improve a process that you don't have complete visibility into and control over.

To eliminate waste and reduce complexity, you need to accurately determine the effectiveness of each and every campaign you launch. That starts with knowing what to measure, how to measure it, and, crucially, how to put those insights into action. In this chapter, we'll delve into some of the most important KPIs to track.

#124 KNOW THE MOST BENEFICIAL KPIs

KPIs measure success toward achieving a specific business goal. There are KPIs for every aspect of business, but we're going to focus on those that matter to sales and marketing teams, as well as the broader sales cycle. By tracking these metrics, you can gain insight into the effectiveness of your campaigns and identify areas of improvement. With a plethora of metrics you can track, here are the ones that matter the most:

- **Demand generation metrics:** Tracking the quality and number of new leads sheds light on buyers and buying groups engaging with your content throughout their buying journeys, enabling you to quantify the overall performance of your marketing team. More importantly, you need to know where those buyers are coming from so you can gauge the effectiveness of each campaign.

- **Conversion rates:** The ultimate goal of any campaign is to increase conversions, which is why this metric is vital for both sales and marketing teams. It's important to track not only the point at which buyers convert but also the interactions that led them to that point. For example, viewing a blog post does not represent a conversion, but it could be a step toward one.

- **Client acquisition cost (CAC):** Every campaign depends on important budgetary decisions, hence why you need to know how much it costs to acquire a new client through any given channel. CAC is usually compared alongside client lifetime value (CLTV). The higher CLTV is compared to your CAC, the healthier your ROI.

- **Sales cycle length:** Depending on your industry and the complexity of your solutions, B2B sales cycles can last months or even upward of a year. In cases where buying groups involve multiple stakeholders ruminating over high-cost commitments, the extended sales cycle is an inevitability. That said, you should always try to reduce it by streamlining the entire buying journey from awareness to advocacy. In other words, every revenue-generating business function has a direct or indirect impact on sales cycle length.

While the above KPIs are fundamental in any business, they'll be subdivided per function and team, and they'll be interpreted differently by each role and department. Regularly reviewing and adjusting these KPIs as the B2B landscape evolves is important for ensuring their continued relevance.

#125 AVOID WASTING TIME FOCUSING ON VANITY METRICS

Understanding your ROI is vital to gauging the success of any campaign, as well as informing future decision-making. That said, it's easy to be swayed by impressive-looking numbers that, upon closer inspection, don't necessarily translate into revenue growth or brand performance. At best, these so-called "vanity metrics" might give an initial impression of success, but because they're neither actionable nor have any bearing on conversions, they're of minimal use.

Common examples of vanity metrics include the number of website visits and the number of social media followers. For instance, having thousands of website visitors per day might seem like a win, until you realize that your bounce rate is over 55 percent. If no one's sticking around, the number of website visits is therefore irrelevant. Similarly, the number of social media followers is meaningless if said followers aren't engaging with your content.

Focus on the actionable metrics that tie in directly to what you want to achieve with a given campaign. For example, the average time visitors spend on a page is a far better indicator of engagement levels, as are any interactions that lead to conversions. Also remember that not all such interactions result in sales, as is the case with website visits or social media followers from industries or regions that your company doesn't serve.

#126 CONNECT AND CONSOLIDATE YOUR DATA SOURCES

Rapidly expanding data footprints are perhaps one of the greatest challenges marketing teams face as they grapple with a myriad of data from different channels. However, if harnessed correctly, this data can be a gold mine for informed decision-making. The true challenge lies in consolidating these data sources to reach meaningful conclusions.

In an "always-on" culture, clients are perpetually connected, expecting instant responses, gratification, and personalized experiences. Moreover, as the digital ecosystem expands, so too does the volume of data collected. To respond quickly to shifting client sentiments and other changes in the B2B space, it's imperative that marketers are always one step ahead.

To navigate this complex environment, marketing teams need the right technology stack. This includes harmonized dashboards that integrate seamlessly with your CRM, social listening tools, email marketing platforms, and any other valuable sources of marketing data. A lean tech stack is a must, since it's much easier to work with fewer tools and platforms than it is to work with a disparate array of unintegrated solutions.

Connecting and consolidating data sources can improve any marketing strategy. For example, Danone improved the effectiveness of its programmatic video advertising campaigns thanks to a unified media-buying approach. This allowed them to identify and remove wasted spend and avoid overexposing users across campaigns. Given the typically higher advertising costs, such optimizations are arguably even more important in B2B organizations.

#127 DON'T TRY TO TRACK EVERYTHING FOR EVERYONE

Digital marketing is like a vast ocean, and it's easy to get lost in the waves of data. With countless metrics at your fingertips, the temptation to track everything and everyone can be overwhelming. However, doing so quickly becomes a massive drain on resources, especially for smaller companies and startups with tighter budgets.

Firstly, it's vital to understand that not all data is valuable. Organizations inevitably collect data that isn't relevant to their goals. The emphasis should be on targeting and collecting data from the right people and prioritizing the channels they spend the most time on. For instance, you might get the occasional promising lead from Facebook, but it is not worth putting as much energy into that platform if the vast majority of qualified social media leads come from LinkedIn. In another example, imagine an IT consulting firm providing solutions for businesses in the American Midwest. They might get the occasional client from the South, who isn't concerned by the distance factor, but they probably don't represent the company's typical target audience. Similar clients may still be worth targeting, but only if your budget allows it.

Deprioritizing or even ignoring data from certain sources might sound disconcerting, but it's a must when resources are limited. However, doing so will help you focus on the target demographics and channels that bring in the most revenue, and it will help streamline your analysis process by reducing digital noise.

#128 IDENTIFY CORRELATIONS BETWEEN STRATEGIES AND COSTS

To know which metrics, channels, and target audiences to track, you need to understand the relationship between individual marketing campaigns and their associated costs and ROIs. By identifying these correlations, you can optimize your budgeting and ensure higher revenue and business growth.

Most businesses have multiple marketing campaigns running simultaneously. However, even if all of them generate demand, not all of those prospective buyers will be of equal value. Some strategies may bring in a high volume of low-quality leads, while others might attract fewer but more suitable prospects. By correlating the cost of each strategy with the value of the deals they close, you can pinpoint which initiatives offer the best value for money and, therefore, which ones to prioritize in future iterations.

A common mistake is to view cost optimization entirely through the lens of reducing costs, but what it is really about is maximizing the value derived from every dollar spent. Consider an example of a B2B tech company that offers cloud services and has a monthly marketing budget of $10,000 distributed across social media, pay-per-click (PPC) advertising, content marketing, and email marketing. After a quarter, they analyze their results:

- **Social media** brought in 50 leads, costing an average of $100 per lead
- **PPC campaigns** brought in 40 leads, costing $150 per lead
- **Content marketing** generated 30 leads, costing $80 per lead
- **Email marketing**, however, secured 80 leads at just $50 per lead

Although in our example the email marketing campaign had the lowest reach (since emails are only sent to prospects who have already opted in for business communications), it has by far the best cost-per-lead ratio. That is not to say the company should neglect its other advertising channels, but it may be worth reallocating more of their budget to email campaigns, especially if their top goal is to onboard more clients.

#129 INVEST IN REDUCING CLIENT ACQUISITION COSTS

While acquiring new clients is vital for business growth, it's just as important to ensure that the cost of acquiring them does not outweigh their value. Reducing client acquisition costs (CAC) not only boosts profitability but also drives more sustainable growth, especially during times of economic uncertainty. Once you have identified the optimal areas for cost-reduction, follow these steps to reduce CAC:

- **Optimize your marketing channels:** As we discussed previously, not all marketing channels yield the same ROI. Regularly assessing the performance of each channel will reveal which ones to prioritize in terms of budgeting.
- **Focus on improving quality:** Rather than casting a wide net, focus on targeting buyers and buying groups that best fit your ICPs. Doing so will increase the likelihood of a conversion, thus reducing CAC. However, remember to regularly review the relevance of your ICPs too.
- **Enhance client onboarding processes:** The sooner new clients start gaining value from your solutions, especially in the case of trial or lower-tier (basic) subscriptions, the more likely they are to stay, thus increasing their value and effectively lowering CAC.
- **Invest in full-funnel content marketing:** Content shouldn't only target prospective buyers; it should also cater to current clients by providing the support they need to obtain maximum value from your products.
- **Launch referral programs:** Your existing clients are potentially your most valuable marketing resource, so offering incentives for referring new business is a great way to cut acquisition costs, as word-of-mouth marketing is often entirely free.

Investing in these strategies doesn't just reduce acquisition costs; it also enhances client relationships and improves the overall quality of your marketing programs, thus leading to sustainable growth and profitability.

#130 TRACK THE IMPACT OF COMMUNITY ENGAGEMENT

In an era of automation and artificial intelligence, it has never been more important for marketers to remember the value of the human touch. While we more often associate communities with consumer-facing brands, they're every bit as important in B2B. Indeed, a hallmark of a successful brand is not just its growth and revenue, but the community of loyal clients that it builds up. As businesses strive to foster genuine connections with their clients, understanding the impact of community engagement becomes paramount. Tracking the impact of community engagement drives organic growth and brand loyalty. It is also a valuable channel for real-time feedback, giving you insights into how you can improve your products, services, or campaigns directly from those who matter most: your clients. With that in mind, here are some key community engagement metrics to track:

- **Engagement rates:** Measure the degree of interaction people have with your branded content, particularly shares and comments, and correlate them with the total number of members in that community.
- **Active members:** These are people who engage in a meaningful way with your content, as opposed to those who might follow you on social media but hardly ever interact with your brand.
- **Community growth rate:** A healthy community, whether it's a social media page, forum, or blog with comments by readers, should have a steady growth trajectory. However, monitoring growth rate alone is insufficient; it is also essential to assess the percentage of members who remain active.
- **Sentiment analysis:** While your team should always take the time to manually evaluate feedback wherever possible, sentiment analysis tools can give you a big-picture view of how each community "feels" about your brand.

Community marketing is a relatively new frontier in B2B marketing and demand generation, but it's an important one. It's not about traditional metrics but understanding the nuances of community dynamics in a world where genuine connections are all the harder to achieve (and maintain).

#131 MONITOR WEBSITE-SOURCED PIPELINE VELOCITY

When it comes to demand generation, the ultimate goal is twofold: to amplify revenue growth in a scalable manner while simultaneously reducing acquisition costs. This dual focus ensures that businesses expand their client base in a way that is financially sustainable and profitable.

The concept of pipeline velocity is central to this endeavor, especially when sourced from your website itself. While revenue remains the ultimate indicator of a business's performance by focusing on the money flowing in, pipeline velocity offers a more nuanced view of the efficacy of your demand generation campaigns. To that end, it encapsulates several essential factors: the win rate, annual contract value (ACV), and the total number of qualified opportunities. By juxtaposing these elements against the sales cycle length, you can garner a comprehensive understanding of how quickly prospective buyers become revenue-generating clients.

Pipeline Velocity = win rate x annual contract value x total qualified opportunities / sales cycle length

While it's normal for B2B sales cycles to be longer than those in B2C, especially where more expensive and complex products are involved, a robust pipeline velocity sourced from your own website is indicative of a healthy demand generation campaign. This approach is among the most cost-effective and easiest to measure, not least because you have complete control over your website, and it is accessible around the clock. As a direct communication channel for your prospective clients, it should also serve as the focal point for the entire buyer journey.

#132 IMPLEMENT MULTI-TOUCH ATTRIBUTION MODELS

No matter how hard you strive to shape a streamlined and seamless buyer journey, that journey will still likely take place across many devices and touchpoints before resulting in a conversion. However, to craft more personalized client experiences, marketing teams need to know which touchpoints resulted in a desired action from their buyers and buying groups. This is why multi-touch attribution models are required, which allow values to be assigned to channels that hold greater weight in the sales process. By contrast, traditional attribution models, such as "last click," attribute the entire conversion value to the last touchpoint the prospect interacted with before converting. While this provides insight into what drove the prospect to make their final decision, it overlooks the cumulative impact of all previous interactions, such as reading blog posts or downloading gated content.

The benefit of multi-touch attribution models is that they distribute conversion value across all touchpoints, ensuring that every interaction gets its due credit. Moreover, equipped with insights into how people interact with various touchpoints, you can continually enhance client experiences and avoid falling into the trap of over-investing in a specific channel.

#133 CRAFT CAMPAIGN PERFORMANCE REPORTS TO INFORM FUTURE INITIATIVES

Every campaign is an opportunity to collect actionable insights to guide future iterations and increase performance. Observable data, particularly on audience characteristics and behavior, is also invaluable for guiding client-facing teams. Paired with set performance criteria, this data establishes a feedback loop that enriches your demand intelligence.

Therefore, it is crucial to implement clear and reliable reporting processes, ensuring data from multiple departments is fed into a single analytics system operating through a demand intelligence lens. Centralizing this information into a single source of truth, as previously discussed, fosters a data-driven culture wherein teams can freely share insights, bolstering performance.

Make sure your performance indicators are tracked in an appropriate time frame, particularly in the case of long-term brand-to-demand plays. In addition to KPIs, pool feedback from client-facing teams, such as sales and client success, to identify high-performing assets and content gaps. AI-augmented analysis of the compiled data can empower and streamline optimizations, informing your marketing campaigns, content strategies, messaging, and even your UVP/USP to ensure resonance with the audience.

#134 KEEP AN EYE ON COMPETITOR PERFORMANCE

While assessing your own performance metrics is crucial, it is equally important to cast an eye on what your competitors are doing and how well they are doing it. This is especially the case in highly competitive and rapidly evolving fields like SaaS. Monitoring the successes and failures of your competitors also helps you identify gaps in your own strategies and identify new competitive differentiators.

For example, if a competitor launches a new product that rapidly gains traction, it could indicate a new market demand that you might also be well positioned to address.

By monitoring competitors' KPIs, you can refine and differentiate your strategies, identify new market opportunities, and anticipate competitive moves and potential threats. Of course, it's not as easy to evaluate your competitors' performance in terms of raw numbers and figures, but the following KPIs can be extremely beneficial:

- **Website traffic and engagement:** Use tools like Alexa or Similar Web to gain insights into competitors' traffic, engagement levels, and even likely sources of traffic.
- **Social media presence and engagement:** Keep an eye on what your competitors are doing on LinkedIn and other relevant networks by using tools like Brandwatch and Social Blade.
- **Client reviews and feedback:** Regularly keep track of people's perceptions about your competitors by tracking reviews on platforms like Trustpilot, G2, and TrustRadius.
- **Product and service offerings:** Keep tabs on your competitors' product updates, new releases, and pricing models to identify any potential market gaps.
- **Search engine and generative engine rankings:** Use tools like Semrush and Ahrefs to see how competitors' websites are performing in relation to your own and gain insights into their SEO/GEO/AEO tactics.

By keeping a finger on the pulse of your competition, you can navigate your market with informed confidence and, in doing so, continuously tailor your campaigns to retain their impact in even the most competitive niches.

CHAPTER 11

DRIVING CONTINUOUS OPTIMIZATION WITH DATA ANALYTICS

We know that data is the lifeblood of any successful marketing strategy, offering a window into everything from client behavior to preferences and sentiments. Even so, knowing what data to collect isn't enough: you also need to think about *how* you are going to collect it and use it to stay ahead of the curve. Over 80 percent of marketers claim that most of their decisions are data-driven, but how effective those decisions are depends on how effectively data is collected and interpreted.

In the previous chapter, we looked at the importance of tracking the metrics that drive informed decision-making and indicate genuine successes (or failures). Now it is time to put those KPIs into use with advanced data analytics and performance optimization strategies, such as A/B testing, cohort analyses, and automated bidding in paid advertising. We will also look at some of the data collection techniques and privacy and compliance essentials that every sales and marketing team should know to succeed.

#135 LEVERAGE PREDICTIVE ANALYTICS TO ANTICIPATE FUTURE TRENDS

Predictive analytics draws upon historical data to forecast future outcomes, helping companies stay ahead in their strategies. However, it is not just about forecasting, but also about interpreting the patterns within massive datasets to make informed decisions. For example, by analyzing past behaviors and purchase histories, you can proactively determine which type of clients are most likely to convert.

This approach is known as lead and account scoring, which we touched on in previous chapters. However, using predictive analytics to inform scoring models is one of the most effective ways to determine who your MQLs and MQAs really are. Moreover, unlike conventional static models, predictive lead scoring is dynamic, adapting whenever new data becomes available. This means scoring is updated in real time, ensuring that sales and marketing teams are basing their decisions on the most current data.

The most advanced approach to lead and account scoring also involves correlating between patterns found in both your first-party data and that of third-party trends. For instance, a prospective buyer might engage in a specific behavior on your company's website. On its own, however, this might not be a strong indicator of their likelihood to convert, but, when correlated to third-party market trends and intent data, it could hold more weight. Remember, predictive scoring isn't about scoring prospects or accounts based on isolated interactions. Instead, it's about contextualizing those interactions within the broader market landscape.

#136 USE SENTIMENT ANALYSIS TO DETERMINE HOW PEOPLE FEEL ABOUT YOUR BRAND

Sentiment analysis, also known as opinion mining, is a method of gauging public sentiment toward your brand, products, or services. Prior to the development of modern analytics tools, the only way to do this was by reading client reviews or fielding feedback directly by way of client satisfaction surveys. While it's still important to maintain manual oversight, it's much harder to scale, which is why such tools are essential for getting insights into your overall audience.

Sentiment analysis is typically an automated process that involves collecting and analyzing feedback at scale using social listening tools. These tools can scrape content from thousands of social media posts, user reviews, and community forums. Then, they use natural language processing (NLP) and AI to identify recurring patterns and themes in that huge corpus of text to answer the question of how your target audience feels about your brand. We mentioned sentiment analysis earlier , and its various types are:

- **Fine-grained analysis:** This relatively basic model measures the polarity of text on a scale following three or more categories (typically negative, neutral, and positive). This can be helpful for studying reviews and ratings at scale.
- **Aspect sentiment analysis:** While it can be helpful to quantify the overall sentiment your clients have about your brand or product, you also need to identify precisely what they like and dislike about it. That is where aspect sentiment comes in by helping you determine the specific aspects or features people are talking about.
- **Emotion detection:** A more advanced model, which requires automation to yield the best results, emotion detection involves detecting a range of emotions by analyzing the tone of text content. We recommend in this case using advanced machine learning solutions, rather than basic lexicons, since people communicate emotion in a myriad of ways.

To implement sentiment analysis effectively, you ideally need a blend of all the above. Choose software that uses AI and machine learning to provide in-depth insights from large amounts of data. Popular options include HubSpot's Service Hub, Idiomatic, Talkwalker, and Reputation. Regardless of which tool you choose, it is essential to integrate multiple first and third-party data sources for maximum effectiveness and accuracy.

#137 PERFORM A/B TESTING TO OPTIMIZE LANDING PAGES AND EMAILS

A/B testing, also known as "split testing," involves comparing two versions of an email, landing page, ad copy or other marketing elements to determine which one performs better. By making incremental changes to the version that performs best, marketers can continuously refine their campaigns. A variation of A/B testing is multivariate testing, in which more than two versions of the campaign run in parallel. Regular A/B testing is straightforward to implement. In the steps below, we'll use a product landing page as an example:

1. **Create two versions of the landing page**, each featuring the different design elements or content you wish to test. With the help of A/B testing software, such as Optimizely or AB Tasty, the version a visitor sees is chosen at random.

2. **Determine which version achieved the most conversions.** Create a copy of this high-performing version and then change a single element. For example, this element could be the size or color of the call-to-action button, the wording of the headline, or the placement of an image.

3. **Repeat the process** by continuously iterating on the best-performing versions of the landing page. It's generally best to make larger changes earlier on in the process, as some trial and error is inevitable. Make smaller iterations as you refine your content.

A/B testing is a methodical process, and the simplest way to do it is to test one variable at a time. If you change multiple elements, especially during later iterations, it will become difficult to determine which one had the highest impact. Finally, ensure you have a large enough sample size so that the results are statistically significant and not just attributable to chance.

#138 OPTIMIZE YOUR PRICING STRATEGY BASED ON CLIENT DEMOGRAPHICS

In chapter 1, we talked about the role of audience demographics and behavioral analytics in informing marketing decisions. These insights can also inform pricing strategies. Optimized pricing gives sales and marketing teams more flexibility when offering solutions to their target audiences, therefore giving it a fundamental role in RevOps alignment.

Start by analyzing the demographic data of your target market, particularly financial behaviors and purchasing power. In the case of B2B, this includes annual revenue, profit and loss, and recent investment rounds. While only public companies typically publish their annual profit and loss statements, you should still be able to get a reasonably accurate picture using a database like Crunchbase or ZoomInfo.

Equipped with these insights, you can tailor your pricing models appropriately. For example, if your research indicates that one segment of your audience has more purchasing power, consider introducing a premium version of your product with additional features and benefits. Conversely, if another segment consists of companies with lower budgets, offering a basic plan that delivers the most value for their investment could be an effective strategy.

Your sales and marketing teams should offer incentives with strategic pricing plans. For instance, when nudging buyers toward conversion, especially those close to making a purchase decision, introducing a tailored offer can be particularly effective. This could come in the form of an early-bird discount, a bundle, or a reduced rate for a longer-term commitment.

Finally, be sure to avoid mismatched pricing. Common pitfalls to avoid include pricing solutions too high, thereby resulting in potential clients perceiving it as unobtainable. On the other hand, pricing a product too low can result in it being perceived as lower quality compared to competitors. After all, quality B2B clients tend to care more about value through the ROI of a solution than pricing itself.

#139 IDENTIFY CROSS-SELLING AND UPSELLING OPPORTUNITIES WITH DATA

Cross-selling and upselling, when augmented with data analytics, are powerful strategies for maximizing CLTV. By taking a deep dive into client behavior, intent, purchase histories, and feedback, you can find opportunities to cross-sell products or upsell premium versions to existing clients. However, it's vital that you take a methodical approach backed up by quality data, since a lack of one or the other can easily backfire to the point of churn.

To ensure your cross-selling and upselling offers are suitably targeted, you need to understand which clients are likely to be most receptive to them. For example, if a client of a software company regularly purchases extra licenses, you might offer an enterprise-level subscription that supports a higher head count at a more economic price. In another case, a client might have a clear need for additional modules or services during certain times of year, at which point you could offer a time-sensitive discount for a premium subscription.

Marketers should also develop data-informed email sequences that address their audience's current pain points. Let's say you're trying to cross-sell a content creation service, for instance. In this case, your first email might highlight the challenges of producing content at scale, while the next could showcase results achieved by similar clients. Finally, you can add a tailored offer in a way that's compelling without being intrusive.

Remember, cross-selling and upselling are not all about getting more money out of your clients. It is even more important to deliver such genuine value to them that they'll be more likely to renew their subscriptions or purchase more from you in the future. In B2B, it's essential to think of these strategies as long-term investments. In fact, upselling and cross-selling might even result in reduced revenue for a period, but that is fine if it increases CLTV by retaining clients for longer.

#140 TWEAK YOUR PAID ADVERTISING SPEND

With third-party cookies being phased out and the demand for personalized user experiences higher than ever, optimizing paid advertising spend has become significantly harder. The role of data analytics in guiding investments is now all the more important.

Optimizing paid advertising spend starts with understanding your CLTV. Top-tier companies are now adept in using data to accurately predict how much revenue they can expect a given client to generate over their lifetime. This insight helps marketers adjust their ad bids to ensure they're still targeting the right users, even though the amount of information they can glean about them from third parties is more limited than it used to be.

As always, however, having a wealth of data is not enough. You also need a complete overview of your marketing data, hence the importance of connecting and consolidating your data sources (as discussed in chapter 10). This helps you fill in the gaps left by the lack of third-party tracking data and identify certain patterns that indicate high-value clients.

Modern digital advertising platforms, such as Google Ads and Adroll, use AI to adjust bids in real time to prioritize high-value targets and spend less on low-value ones. These processes draw upon a myriad of data points, including time of day, location, and purchasing behaviors.

#141 IMPROVE CLIENT ONBOARDING EXPERIENCES

Once a client has made a purchase, the next phase involves promoting brand evangelism. This begins with the onboarding process, which, in the case of many B2B services, might span weeks or even months. For example, a complex product like an enterprise resource planning (ERP) system typically takes three to nine months for a small business to implement, and twice that time for large enterprises. Of course, the sooner your newest clients can start gaining maximum value out of your product, the better; however, the quality of the onboarding experience is also critical.

Initial onboarding experiences set the tone for the entire client relationship, so it's important to take an informed, data-driven approach from the outset. For example, if your data reveals that a certain client segment shows interest in a particular feature, then the onboarding process should highlight it. Conversely, having an onboarding process that focuses on features a client is not likely to use may increase friction and tarnish the user experience, increasing the risk of churn.

Data analytics offer vital insight into how users interact with a product during the onboarding phase. By identifying potential issues early on, client experience teams can make adjustments to improve the process. This is important for sales teams too, especially in cases where client onboarding begins before a sale is actually made, as is the case with trial and demo versions. For instance, if your data indicates users are getting stuck on a particular step while getting acquainted with your product, you can implement changes to keep them from dropping out of the funnel or, in the case of paying clients, abandoning you completely.

#142 CONDUCT A COHORT ANALYSIS FOR DEEPER INSIGHT

A cohort analysis is an advanced form of behavioral analytics whereby you take a group of clients who share certain traits and analyze their usage patterns to better understand their actions. In this case, a cohort refers to the specific group of users with those shared characteristics. There are two types of cohort analysis of most interest to B2B organizations:

- **Acquisition cohorts** are groups divided based on when they converted. Their shared characteristics help you measure retention and churn rates over a given period. For a B2B

SaaS company, an identifying characteristic could be their sign-up date.

- **Behavioral cohorts** are groups divided based on how they interact with your product. This lets you analyze active users from specific demographics and behavioral patterns. For example, a uniting characteristic might be the use of a certain product feature.

The power of cohort analysis lies in its ability to give you a granular view of your clients. For instance, analyzing churn rates across the board for a given month is of little value, but, by conducting a cohort analysis, you can pinpoint exactly which clients are churning, as well as when and why.

Consider using both types of cohort analysis to garner insight into how you're attracting new clients and how you're retaining them. These methods of analysis provide detailed insights into important metrics throughout a client's tenure with your business. For example, a horizontal analysis can help you gauge how retention develops over time, while a vertical approach can shed light on retention during specific periods of the client relationship for a given cohort.

#143 MAKE SENSE OF BIG DATA WITH DATA VISUALIZATION TOOLS

From website traffic patterns to CRM databases, marketers are inundated with increasingly enormous datasets that are impossible to make sense of through manual means alone. On average, data volumes are growing by two thirds every month, and the mean number of data sources per enterprise has increased to four hundred. The only way for such quantities of data to be useful is to apply machine learning and artificial intelligence to distill it down into bite-size insights. Enter the mission-critical role of data visualization tools.

People are visual creatures, hence the importance of data visualization. Tools like Microsoft Power BI and Tableau allow users across business departments, sales and marketing included, to gain quick insights into vast amounts of data. By using AI and machine learning to analyze data at scale, detect patterns, and predict future trends, these tools represent data points and insights in graphs, charts, and various other visual formats, without the need for a large team of data scientists.

When choosing a data visualization tool, your number one priority should be integrability with your existing data sources. Leading solutions have hundreds of connectors available, making them adaptable enough for use in a broad range of environments. However, as we mentioned in chapter 10, it can be enormously helpful to consolidate your existing data sources into as lean a tech stack as possible. After all, the accuracy and relevance of your data visualizations depend entirely on how orderly your datasets are.

#144 INCORPORATE DATA PRIVACY BY DESIGN AND DEFAULT

In an age when every digital activity can be tracked and recorded, it's no surprise that privacy has become an evolving concern in the past decade. For B2B enterprises, privacy isn't just about staying on the right side of the law; it's also about building and preserving trust at a time when the trust deficit is at an all-time high. Almost three quarters of people do not trust companies to safeguard their privacy by using their personal data exclusively with their permission.

This is a critical issue, especially given the importance of trust and transparency in B2B relationships. That is why this chapter concludes with an emphasis on incorporating privacy by design and default in all of your data collection, management, and analytics efforts. While every company needs data to inform marketing, sales, finance, and other operations, it is vital that your processes be both transparent and compliant.

Most importantly, all marketing must be permission-based. Data privacy and security are not afterthoughts to be acted on later. Instead, they should be integral to every tool and strategy you adopt, from email marketing to social media. Moreover, you should only actively collect data that is necessary for the task in question. Data minimization is not just a lawful imperative; it is also a best practice to maintain the quality of your datasets.

Finally, make sure your data is stored and managed in such a way that you can easily reveal all personally identifiable data you have about a given individual. Laws like CCPA and GDPR grant people the right to submit subject access requests (SARs), and companies must respond within thirty days. This is a much easier process when you have robust data management processes in place, along with the foundational principles of privacy by design.

CHAPTER 12

STAYING AHEAD OF THE CURVE IN DIGITAL MARKETING

In the ever-evolving world of digital marketing, the only constant is change. The tools and strategies that work today might not be the best choice tomorrow, and as technology advances and economies fluctuate, consumer behaviors shift along with them. New challenges and opportunities arise all the time, and often without warning.

One of the most pervasive trends currently shaping the future of B2B marketing is the growing adoption of AI, the global market for which is expected to reach a value of $310 billion by 2026. However, the sudden proliferation of AI has brought new concerns regarding privacy, content quality, and legislative control.

Throughout this book, we have explored some of the most effective digital marketing strategies in use today. By putting them into action, you will set a robust foundation for a sustainable marketing program that is well-equipped to adapt to ever-changing market pressures. But it is also important to keep an eye on the future, which is why we are going to dedicate this chapter to our biggest predictions for the B2B marketing world in the years ahead.

#145   BE WARY OF FREEZING CAMPAIGNS DURING PERIODS OF ECONOMIC UNCERTAINTY

When facing periods of economic uncertainty, most businesses instinctively look for ways to cut costs, and marketing budgets are often the first to face the axe. However, this approach is counterproductive, especially when it comes to demand generation and driving long-term brand awareness.

Remember that marketing is not just about increasing visibility. It is also about building relationships, maintaining trust, and asserting industry authority. These factors are arguably even more important during times of economic downturn, as they are often accompanied by a decrease in buyer confidence. This is where value-adding content, which helps clients get more out of your products and services, shines its brightest. By offering real value and support to your existing and potential client base, you can continue showcasing the solutions that they need more than ever.

Sometimes, of course, budget cuts are unavoidable. It's also true that some campaigns might not be as effective during a recession. In this case, the best approach is to reconfigure them and revisit your marketing messages to ensure they're better suited to the times. Quality over quantity is fundamental here, so, especially with strategies like content marketing, it's much better to publish fewer pieces, albeit highly targeted ones, than lots of low-effort content.

When funds are few, it's vital to budget strategically. Be sure to base every decision on good data to know where to invest and where to cut back. If your business offers multiple related products, you might also consider promoting them together to reduce costs and make them more appealing to prospective clients.

#146 INVEST IN ARTIFICIAL INTELLIGENCE, BUT BE WARY OF THE HYPE

The potential of AI in marketing automation is undeniable. However, so too are the risks of overreliance. Among the most common concerns are saturation and the potential loss of the human touch, particularly where generative AI solutions like Midjourney and ChatGPT are concerned.

In analytics, AI-powered solutions have become a practical necessity in analyzing huge datasets. However, the usefulness of data analytics is inherently limited by the quality of the data it analyzes. If your data sources are inconsistent or outdated, you'll end up with misleading insights, biases, and other issues.

The importance of the human touch cannot be overstated. For example, when a potential client has a query about a solution that a chatbot cannot address, they are unlikely to be satisfied with a generic, automated reply. Similarly, existing clients seeking support expect personalized and effective solutions, some of which demand a human touch. While automated solutions generate quick responses to simple queries, they fall short when handling complex or emotionally charged situations that require human understanding.

Whether it's using AI to automate content marketing processes, support data-driven decision-making, or other strategies, it is vital to maintain a human element of control. View AI as a way to augment team members' abilities and free up time for them to focus on what they do best, whether that is engaging buyers and buying groups in one-to-one conversation or nurturing existing clients with impeccable support.

#147 EMPHASIZE AI AUGMENTATION OVER CONTENT CREATION

The release of OpenAI's ChatGPT in late 2022 ushered in an unprecedented AI boom, with many companies rushing to adopt the technology in hopes of being the first to fully leverage its untapped potential. This development quickly pushed AI to reach the point the Gartner Hype Cycle terms the "peak of inflated expectations." Consequently, while four out of five business leaders consider AI a business imperative to maintain a competitive edge, three out of five admit their organization lacks a congruent vision for AI implementation, in addition to demonstrating concerns regarding the quantification of AI's impact on productivity.

Attempts at cutting costs by automating content creation led to a flood of low-quality AI-generated content, impacting buyer experience. The sheer quantity of this content overwhelmed buyers conducting independent research, highlighting the importance and value of content that offers true thought leadership and actionable insights. In spite of these developments, 72 percent of marketers still predominantly utilize AI for content creation, in stark contrast to the 18 percent of buyers who plan to use it for content creation.

It is therefore imperative for marketers to pivot to more strategic AI uses, which augment and optimize existing processes and glean powerful insights from prospect data to support performance. AI can also be leveraged by marketers to facilitate personalization at scale. Combined, these uses have the potential to drive unparalleled experiences, custom-tailored to each member of a buying group, fueling data-driven buyer enablement approaches capable of achieving truly remarkable outcomes.

#148 FOCUS ON UTILIZING AI TOOLS THAT DELIVER MEASURABLE IMPACT OVER SPECULATIVE APPLICATIONS

As companies move away from a growth-at-all-costs approach to utilizing AI, teams have been tasked with implementing these systems with greater strategic vision and pivoting away from ad hoc applications.

The State of B2B

GROWTH AT ALL COSTS
- Post-pandemic revival
- PE/VC-driven
- SaaS model thrives

GTM IS THE NEW DEMAND
- The rise of the partnership ecosystem
- Digital transformation 2.0
- Ultra-precision with data intelligence
- Buyer scrutiny ABM evolves into ABX

2022 **2023** **2024** **2025**

RIGHT-SIZING TECH
- Fear of recession pauses spend
- PE/VC drying up pauses spend
- AI hype cycle pauses spend
- Buying committees in a defensive position

AI-DRIVEN INNOVATION AND GROWTH
- GTM teams align for tech transformation
- AI is the top investment focus
- Brand-to-demand strategies drive buyer engagement
- Services-as-a-software model is born

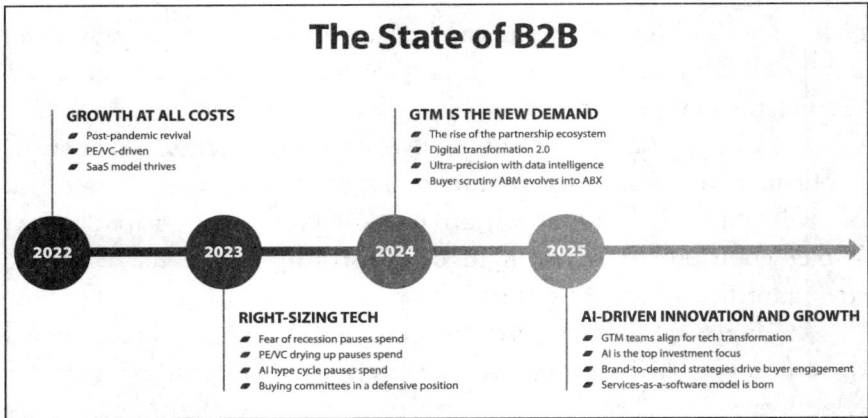

Although about 70 percent of buyers are still looking to adopt new AI solutions, investments are now being made focusing on potential contribution to the bottom line. Speculative, experimental applications are being discarded as companies strive to leverage AI systems to boost interdepartmental, strategic outcomes. Therefore, identifying AI systems that not only demonstrate significant, measurable impact, but provide transformative capabilities has become crucial.

By offering highly scalable personalization and predictive data analysis, effective AI implementations go beyond a single department to augment the capabilities of multiple teams, from marketing and sales to product development and client success. This provides support for the entirety of the buyer's journey and contributes to bringing long-term goals to fruition. Conversely, ad hoc AI adoption, lacking full organizational alignment and a strategic vision, is likely to exacerbate existing challenges across business operations.

#149 KEEP CLOSE TRACK OF EVOLVING AI LEGISLATION

For the past few years, data privacy regulations have been discussed, proposed, and amended multiple times by governmental entities across the world. These laws are now consolidated up to a point in which full compliance is expected from companies internationally, lest they incur serious fines and reputational damage. However, the popularization and iterative development of AI systems ushered in a series of new debates concerning these systems' usage of different types of data in their training and development, especially considering the sheer scale in which AI tools can harvest and leverage data.

As tech giants Google, Meta, OpenAI, and others all risked hitting a wall in the development of their AI models, due to having scraped nearly all publicly available online data, all three companies adopted strategies veering into gray areas in copyright law. OpenAI, for example, developed and deployed Whisper, a speech recognition system, to transcribe over one million hours of content from YouTube to fuel its GPT. Google, YouTube's proprietor, despite initially seeking to take legal action in response, would soon have to resort to similar measures. The copyrights to YouTube content, however, are held by its respective creators. Consequently, both Google and Meta edited their privacy policies to be more lenient regarding the usage of publicly available user data to train their AI systems.

As a result, the datasets used to train AI increasingly contained sensitive, personally identifiable, and copyrighted information, which made them prime targets for cybercriminals and increased the potential damage in case of leaks. The increased scrutiny of and demand for ethical AI usage culminated in government agencies issuing policies such as the 2024 EU Artificial Intelligence Act, to enforce specific risk management, data governance, and use case regulations.

As an iterative technology, AI evolves exponentially, making it a driving force for new policies and regulations as updates are released. This makes it imperative for your teams to keep close track of evolving AI regulations to ensure compliance. Having fully compliant data privacy and user consent mechanisms in place prior to AI implementation can ease this process.

#150 EXPLORE THE POSSIBILITIES OF NEUROMARKETING AND SEMIOTICS

Neuromarketing and semiotics are approaches inspired by psychology and linguistics to analyze behavioral factors of your target audience. While neuromarketing focuses on understanding the brain's responses to marketing stimuli, semiotics examines the signs and symbols in content and how people interpret them. Together, they offer a powerful way to create compelling marketing campaigns.

Neuromarketing requires a pragmatic approach, ensuring that both the language and design of your content resonate with its intended audience. In other words, it is not just about what you say, but how you say it. That is where semiotics comes in, with its focus on how the visual elements of a campaign, such as the color schemes and imagery used, support messaging by evoking certain emotions or associations in different audiences.

For example, one of the key features of Amazon's logo is an arrow that stretches from the letter A to Z, representing the idea that they sell everything from A to Z. This logo also represents a smiley face, therefore promoting a message of client satisfaction and positivity—both highly beneficial as a brand image. The semiotic process, as conceptualized by psychologists and philosophers like Piaget and Kant, involves defining the intended message, determining how to best represent that message, and predicting how the audience might interpret it.

To harness neuromarketing and semiotics effectively, you need to consider factors such as emotional resonance and cultural sensitivity. For example, blue tends to symbolize high quality and professionalism in Western societies, while purple and even green or yellow have a similar cultural resonance in China, Japan, and Korea. In a different context, blue often denotes an upward trend and red a downward trend in the US and Europe, but the reverse is the case in much of Asia.

Ultimately, the integration of neuromarketing and semiotics in your campaigns offers a more nuanced approach to marketing. As advanced tools like sentiment analysis and heatmapping become more affordable, it is almost certain that these tactics will become increasingly popular and accessible in B2B marketing.

#151 FOCUS ON AGILE PROJECT MANAGEMENT FOR GREATER ADAPTABILITY

Businesses no longer have the luxury of time on their side when it comes to marketing and sales. Today, the ability to adapt quickly to sudden, and often unexpected, changes in the market is essential. That is where agile project management comes in.

Agile project management focuses on driving business action, adaptability, and feedback loops. Tech teams have been embracing the agile methodology for years, since it prevents them from getting caught up in long planning cycles.

While B2C sectors have been quick to adopt the agile approach in marketing, the B2B world, known for its caution, has been slower on the uptake. However, given the equally dynamic nature of B2B sales and marketing, agile presents a unique opportunity for businesses to future-proof their operations. By adopting an agile methodology, you'll be able to roll out new campaigns quickly, gather real-time feedback, and tweak strategies in short and focused cycles.

For best results, consider adopting the Scrum approach. Scrum is a popular agile methodology among tech teams due to its emphasis on teamwork, adaptability, and short productivity bursts known as "sprints." All those factors are important in sales and marketing too, especially in a RevOps-optimized environment.

For example, when applied in sales and marketing, the team might dedicate one sprint to launching an email campaign, during which they design, test, and send out the emails and gather feedback. In the next sprint, the team reviews the campaign's performance, learns from its successes and failures, and applies these insights to the next iteration. In this case, each sprint encompasses an iterative improvement on the previous one, based on feedback, and within a clear time frame.

B2B clients expect open dialogue and transparency. By bridging the responsiveness and trust gap between brands and audiences, the agile methodology supports this ethos and delivers continuous value.

#152 BUILD UP EMPLOYEES' RESILIENCE TO CHANGE

Disruptive events, such as global pandemics, wars, and trade policy uncertainties, have underscored the need for adaptability, and that starts with your team. In a 2022 report on the trends and priorities of HR, Gartner found that almost half of respondents identified change management as a top priority for 2023. This aligns with the finding that most workers feel overwhelmed by the relentless changes they have had to navigate in recent years, such as the sudden shift to remote work (not to mention the sometimes unexpected return to the office). To foster a resilient workforce, Gartner emphasizes three key pillars:

1. **Healthy employees:** Employee well-being is paramount, which is why HR departments and team leaders alike must be vigilant in monitoring signs of stress and burnout. They must actively promote a healthy work-life balance that keeps people performing and feeling at their best.
2. **Healthy relationships:** Any effective workforce is built on a foundation of transparency and trust, and that depends on solid collaboration and communication. Holding regular team-building exercises and listening to feedback is vital to promoting healthy relationships, especially in remote work environments.
3. **Healthy environment:** The physical and cultural environment in which employees work also plays a crucial role in their resilience. With innovative and inclusive workspaces and ample opportunities for professional

growth and development, employees will feel valued in their roles.

It might be tempting to consider these factors the responsibilities of the HR team, but the reality is that everyone, sales and marketing leaders and their team members included, has a role to play in fostering a healthy workplace.

Moreover, as with any business department, the effectiveness of any sales and marketing team depends on the resilience of its workforce. When employees are equipped to handle change resiliently and confidently, they will work happier and smarter. This influences client sentiment too. After all, no sales and marketing initiative is likely to succeed if those behind it lack motivation, belief, and empathy.

#153 PRESERVE BRAND TRUST AND AUTHENTICITY IN AN ERA OF MISINFORMATION

While the rapid dissemination of information certainly has its advantages, it also comes with significant challenges, particularly during periods of economic and geopolitical disruption. The rising tide of misinformation and disinformation in the wake of major events like the COVID pandemic and the wars in Ukraine and the Middle East is a stark reminder of how such campaigns can snowball on social media.

It can be tempting to pin these problems solely on questionable media outlets and malicious actors. However, the reality is that many legitimate organizations are unwittingly funding such efforts. A recent report by NewsGuard and Comscore found that brands collectively spent $2.6 billion in one year on advertising displayed on misinformative news sites. This problem has been greatly accentuated by the complexities of the programmatic advertising industry.

These challenges have a knock-on effect on brand trust and authenticity. In B2B markets, where potential buyers tend to scrutinize every purchase very carefully to ensure their supply chains align with their ESG initiatives, sales and marketing teams need to work hard to preserve trust and secure buy-in.

As misinformation and disinformation campaigns become increasingly sophisticated with the rise of generative AI, businesses must be proactive in protecting their brand's authenticity and trust. This requires ongoing team training and awareness, unified messaging, and stringent oversight across all brand communications.

#154 PRIORITIZE DEMAND GENERATION AS A LONG-TERM STRATEGY

In the dynamic world of B2B, you need an adaptable strategy that can withstand the ebbs and flows of the market. Demand generation lies at the heart of any such sustainable strategy by delivering a holistic process that goes beyond capturing leads to build brand awareness, nurture potential clients, and drive conversions. As you navigate the complexities of an ever-changing market, it's imperative that you prioritize demand generation as a long-term strategy.

In a time of rapid and constant technological development and short-lived hype cycles, it's easy to be seduced by the lure of trends for short-term gains. However, although tactics like trend marketing and limited-time promotions undeniably have their value in certain settings, they are not ideally suited to the longer buying cycles of B2B, which are not subject to the impulse purchases common in B2C markets.

That is why demand generation is a game changer: it drives long-term gain by understanding and catering to the evolving needs of your target audiences, which fosters sustained brand awareness in your market. To make demand strategies work, you need to adopt advanced data analytics, keep a keen eye on industry trends, and acquire a genuine understanding of the pain points and aspirations of your ideal clients (and their buying group members). The right content, tailored to the various stages of the buyer's journey, from awareness to post-purchase, is the linchpin of such a strategy.

Successful demand generation strategies are also fluid, ready to pivot based on shifts in the market and real-time feedback.

This supports an iterative approach, powered by solutions like A/B testing, audience surveys, and social listening. To that end, all your advertising campaigns should fall under the umbrella of a consolidated and adaptable long-term demand generation strategy.

#155 PREPARE FOR CONTINUOUS READJUSTMENTS IN THE TECH MARKET

Even if the COVID pandemic has eased, its ripple effects on the business world continue. Companies had to swiftly adopt tech solutions and boost HR spending to facilitate remote work, leading to unforeseen budget adjustments. Many businesses found themselves with an inflated tech stack due to a rushed digitization. Once again, they have had to reassess their budgets, cut down on redundant expenses, and revisit their strategies.

The pandemic wasn't the first disruption to hit the business world, and it will not be the last. As I write this chapter, significant uncertainties in global trade policies continue to cause ongoing market volatility, in turn pausing many hiring and budget decisions. As geopolitical pressures impact global markets and supply chains, companies must prepare for the unknown. The constantly evolving legislative landscape is another area of concern for businesses. For example, as the EU strives to achieve greater data sovereignty in a world dominated by US-headquartered companies, businesses must be ever more vigilant about their data collection and management processes.

Even B2B companies that don't explicitly consider themselves to be tech businesses need to be ready for this continuing adjustment of the market. With many tech renewals due at the end of each year, businesses across the board are always under pressure in Q4 to showcase the value of their services. They need to constantly emphasize how they can help generate revenue, enhance client satisfaction, and improve productivity. In other words, businesses cannot just position their solutions as being suitable for current market conditions, but as drivers of performance during challenging and unpredictable times.

FINAL THOUGHTS

Navigating the complex world of B2B marketing in these uncertain times is both a challenge and an opportunity. We're equipped with the most sophisticated tools and methodologies we've ever had, allowing us to delve deeply into understanding our target audiences and crafting impactful strategies at scale.

However, this complex environment can act as a double-edged sword. Our competitors are also leveraging these tools, and the risk of our messages becoming overshadowed in the cacophony of digital noise has never been greater. In addition, the growing demands for privacy and transparency in a world where almost everything we do online is tracked (and often not for legitimate reasons) is a significant challenge.

As we've journeyed through this book, we've learned that, with a meticulous and strategic approach, B2B marketers can not only reach their target audiences but also foster meaningful and lasting connections. Of course, it's not all about tools and tactics. It's about understanding, nurturing, and evolving. By focusing on our audience's needs, nurturing with precision, closing deals with finesse, and continuously measuring and optimizing our campaigns, we can set the stage for sustained success.

These strategies and frameworks aren't meant to serve as static blueprints. They should evolve alongside your organization and the shifting dynamics of the market. The most successful B2B marketers treat each campaign as an opportunity to learn and refine, recognizing that what proves effective today may require adjustment tomorrow. This iterative approach isn't a concession to uncertainty: it's a strategic advantage that keeps you responsive and competitive.

In sharing these advanced B2B marketing practices, my hope is that this book has helped you follow a roadmap: one that's been charted by over two decades of experience, insights, and a deep understanding of the nuances of B2B marketing. As you move forward, take these insights, mold them to align with your specific context and circumstances, and innovate continuously. The B2B marketing ecosystem is vast and ever changing, but with the right strategies and an unwavering commitment to excellence, the path to success is well within reach. Here's to your continued growth and triumph!

REFERENCES

"5 Steps to Futureproof Your Demand with First-Party Data Ahead of Cookie Changes," *INFUSE*. (s.d.). Retrieved January 27, 2025, from https://infuse.com/insight/5-steps-cookie-futureproof-b2b-first-party-data/.

"6 Common Attribution Models that Can Demonstrate Marketing's Contribution to Revenue," *DemandGen* (Blog), May 10, 2022. Retrieved March 28, 2024, from https://www.demandgen.com/attribution-models-demonstrating-marketing-contribution-to-revenue/.

"6 Lead Nurturing Strategies for Reaching Beyond the Inbox," *INFUSE*. (n.d.). Retrieved January 31, 2025, from https://infuse.com/insight/6-lead-nurturing-strategies-for-reaching-beyond-the-inbox/.

"6 Steps to Targeting a B2B Buying Group," *INFUSE*. (n.d.). Retrieved March 28, 2024, from https://infuse.com/insight/6-steps-to-marketing-to-a-b2b-buying-group/.

"6 Ways to Revolutionize Your B2B Digital Experience," *INFUSE*. (n.d.). Retrieved March 28, 2024, from https://infuse.com/insight/6-ways-to-revolutionize-your-b2b-digital-experience/.

"10 B2B Digital Marketing Channels for 2022 That Actually Work," *INFUSE*, November 9, 2021. Retrieved March 28, 2024, from https://infuse.com/b2b-marketing-channels/.

"10 High Converting Lead Magnet Examples and Design Ideas," *INFUSE*. (n.d.). Retrieved March 29, 2024, from https://infuse.com/insight/lead-magnet-examples/.

"10 Mistakes to Stop Making in Your Lead Follow-Up," *INFUSE*. (n.d.). Retrieved March 29, 2024, from https://infuse.com/insight/10-mistakes-to-stop-making-in-your-lead-follow-up/.

"10 Sales and Marketing Alignment Best Practices," *INFUSE*, March 21, 2022. Retrieved March 29, 2024, from https://infuse.com/insight/10-sales-and-marketing-alignment-best-practices/.

"10 Simple Ways to Optimize Your Website For Lead Generation," *INFUSE*, March 9, 2022. Retrieved March 28, 2024, from https://infuse.com/insight/optimize-your-website-for-lead-generation/.

"12 Examples of B2B SaaS Apps Using Gamification," *SaaS Designer* (n.d.). Retrieved March 29, 2024, from https://saasdesigner.com/12-examples-of-b2b-saas-apps-using-gamification/.

"13th Annual B2B Content Marketing Benchmarks, Budgets, and Trends," *Content Marketing Institute,* October 19, 2022. Retrieved January 31, 2025, from https://contentmarketinginstitute.com/wp-content/uploads/2022/10/b2b-2023-research-final.pdf.

"30 Examples of Creative Content Marketing Done Right," *INFUSE* (n.d.). Retrieved March 29, 2024, from https://infuse.com/insight/30-examples-of-creative-content-marketing-done-right/.

"The 2024 B2B Buyer Experience Report," *6sense* (n.d.). Retrieved January 27, 2025, from https://6sense.com/science-of-b2b/2024-buyer-experience-report/.

"A/B Testing for B2B Marketers," *MarTech Series,* August 12, 2022. Retrieved March 29, 2024, from https://martechseries.com/mts-insights/staff-writers/a-b-testing-for-b2b-marketers/.

"AI at Work Is Here. Now Comes the Hard Part," 2024 *Work Trend Index Annual Report from Microsoft and LinkedIn,* May 8, 2024. Retrieved January 31, 2025, from https://www.microsoft.com/en-us/worklab/work-trend-index/ai-at-work-is-here-now-comes-the-hard-part.

Albert, V. "The Evolution of the Marketer in 2023," *INFUSE.* (n.d.). Retrieved March 29, 2024, from https://infuse.com/insight/the-evolution-of-the-marketer/.

Alparslan, M. "How Analytics Can Create a Better Onboarding Experience for Your Customers," *Dataroid,* November 3, 2022. Retrieved March 29, 2024, from https://www.dataroid.com/blog/how-analytics-can-create-a-better-onboarding-experience-for-your-customers/.

The Art of ABM: A Strategic Guide to Account-Based Marketing. (n.d.). *Drift.* Retrieved March 28, 2024, from https://www.drift.com/books-reports/account-based-marketing-strategy/.

"Artificial Intelligence (AI) Market by Offering (Hardware, Software), Technology (ML (Deep Learning (LLM, Transformers (GPT 1, 2, 3, 4)), NLP, Computer Vision), Business Function, Vertical, and Region–Global Forecast to 2030," *MarketsandMarkets,* June 2023. Retrieved March 29, 2024, from https://www.marketsandmarkets.com/Market-Reports/artificial-intelligence-market-74851580.html.

"B2B Buying Has Changed. How Should Marketers Respond?" *Forrester,* November 4, 2021. Retrieved March 28, 2024, from https://www.forrester.com/what-it-means/ep242-b2b-buying-study/.

"B2B Buying: How Top CSOs and CMOs Optimize the Journey," *Gartner,* (n.d.). Retrieved March 28, 2024, from https://www.gartner.com/en/sales/insights/b2b-buying-journey.

"B2B Lead Qualification: How to Find MQLs Efficiently in 2023 and Beyond," *INFUSE,* (n.d.). Retrieved March 29, 2024, from https://infuse.com/insight/b2b-lead-qualification-how-to-find-mqls-efficiently/.

"A B2B Marketing Jumpstart to Account-Based Marketing," *LinkedIn Marketing Solutions,* (n.d.). Retrieved March 28, 2024, from https://business.linkedin.com/marketing-solutions/cx/19/10/b2b-marketing-jumpstart-guide-to-abm.

Barba, M., Yarborough, B., Mortenson, C., Rivera, N., Powers, J., Anderson, T., Basu, S., Veerkamp, C., Verwey, D., Medley, J., Stroup, B., Babu, M., Kelley, W., Raleigh, D., III, Manova, K., Hargett, J., Evans, K., Samuel, S., Kelly, M., ... Yap, A. "B2B Expert Roundup: What Is the Link Between RevOps and Client Experience?" *INFUSE*, (n.d.). Retrieved January 31, 2025, from https://infuse.com/insight/b2b-expert-roundup-what-is-the-link-between-revops-and-client-experience/.

Belden, M. "Channel Partner Segmentation: Identifying Emerging Superstars," *Forrester*, (2017, May 19). Retrieved March 29, 2024, from https://www.forrester.com/blogs/channel-partner-segmentation-identifying-emerging-superstars/.

"Best Practices for Hosting a Channel Partner Summit & Other Partner Events," *ITA Group*, (n.d.). Retrieved March 29, 2024, from https://www.itagroup.com/insights/event-marketing/best-practices-hosting-channel-partner-events.

Biderman-Gross, F. "Metrics That Matter: How To Measure Your B2B Marketing Success," *Forbes*, March 17, 2022. Retrieved March 29, 2024, from https://www.forbes.com/sites/forbesagencycouncil/2022/03/17/metrics-that-matter-how-to-measure-your-b2b-marketing-success/?sh=478b16733dca.

Blank, S. "How to Build a Web Startup—Lean LaunchPad Edition," *Steveblank.com*. September 22, 2011. Retrieved March 28, 2024, from https://steveblank.com/2011/09/22/how-to-build-a-web-startup-lean-launchpad-edition/.

"Brand-to-Demand: The Future of B2B Growth," *INFUSE*, (n.d.). Retrieved January 27, 2025, from https://infuse.com/insight/brand-to-demand-future-of-b2b-growth/.

Brenner, M. "Here's Your AI-Based Customer Segmentation Strategy," *Marketing Insider Group*, February 20, 2019. Retrieved March 28, 2024, from https://marketinginsidergroup.com/artificial-intelligence/how-to-improve-customer-segmentation-with-ai/.

Bump, P. "Why Marketers Should Implement User-Generated Content: 23 Stats to Know," *HubSpot*, July 30, 2021. Retrieved March 29, 2024, from https://blog.hubspot.com/marketing/user-generated-content-stats.

"Buyer Advocacy: How to Engage Your Defensive Buying Groups," *INFUSE*, (n.d.). Retrieved January 27, 2025, from https://infuse.com/insight/how-to-engage-defensive-buying-groups/.

Campbell, G. "Demand Marketer's Guide to Intent Activation," *INFUSE*, (n.d.). Retrieved March 28, 2024, from https://infuse.com/insight/demand-marketers-guide-to-intent-activation/.

Clay, R. "Why You Must Follow Up Leads," *Marketing Donut*, (n.d.). Retrieved March 29, 2024, from https://www.marketingdonut.co.uk/sales/sales-strategy/why-you-must-follow-up-leads.

"Customer Segmentation Using Machine Learning," *Javatpoint*, (n.d.). Retrieved March 28, 2024, from https://www.javatpoint.com/customer -segmentation-using-machine-learning.

"The Dangers of Only Focusing on Bottom of Funnel Leads," *INFUSE*, (n.d.). Retrieved March 29, 2024, from https://infuse.com/insight/the -dangers-of-only-focusing-on-bottom-of-funnel-leads/.

"The Dark Side of AI in Marketing: Understating the Disadvantages," *ThinkML*, May 7, 2023. Retrieved March 29, 2024, from https: //thinkml.ai/the-dark-side-of-ai-in-marketing/.

Davies, A. "Seven Benefits of Predictive Analytics for B2B Organizations," *Optimizely*, June 12, 2020. Retrieved March 29, 2024, from https://www .optimizely.com/insights/7-benefits-of-predictive-analytics-for-b2b/.

Dawes, J. "Advertising Effectiveness and the 95-5 Rule: Most B2B Buyers Are Not in the Market Right Now," *The B2B Institute*. (n.d.). Retrieved March 29, 2024, from https://business.linkedin.com/content/dam/me /business/en-us/marketing-solutions/resources/pdfs/advertising -effectiveness-and-the-95-5-rule.pdf.

"Death of the MQL? How to Qualify Prospects in 2025," *INFUSE,* (n.d.). Retrieved January 27, 2025, from https://infuse.com/insight/death-of -mql-how-to-qualify-prospects/.

"Defining Behavioral Segmentation With 7 Examples," *INFUSE*, (n.d.). Retrieved March 28, 2024, from https://infuse.com/insight/behavioral -segmentation-examples/.

"Definitive Guide to B2B Buyer Personas," *INFUSE*, (n.d.). Retrieved March 28, 2024, from https://infuse.com/insight/definitive-guide-to-b2b -buyer-personas/.

"Definitive Guide to B2B Lead Nurturing," *INFUSE*, (n.d.).Retrieved March 29, 2024, from https://infuse.com/insight/definitive-guide-to-b2b -lead-nurturing/.

"Definitive Guide to B2B Market Segmentation," *INFUSE*, (n.d.). Retrieved March 28, 2024, from https://infuse.com/insight/definitive-guide-to-b2b -market-segmentation/.

"Definitive Guide to B2B Psychographics," *INFUSE*, (n.d.). Retrieved March 28, 2024, from https://infuse.com/insight/a-definitive-guide-to -marketing-psychographics/.

"Definitive Guide to the B2B Dark Funnel," *INFUSE*, (n.d.). Retrieved March 29, 2024, from https://infuse.com/blog/insight/definitive-guide-to -the-b2b-dark-funnel/.

"Demographic Segmentation in B2B Marketing: Tips, Insights & Best Practices," *INFUSE*, October 25, 2021. Retrieved March 28, 2024, from https://infuse.com/insight/demographic-segmentation-b2b-marketing/.

Dengsøe, M. "The Hidden Cost of Data Quality Issues on the Return of Ad Spend," *Towards Data Science*, July 6, 2023. Retrieved March 29,

2024, from https://towardsdatascience.com/the-hidden-cost-of-data-quality-issues-on-the-return-of-ad-spend-dd8c99b3289e.

"The Do's and Don'ts of Channel Marketing," *INFUSE*, (n.d.). Retrieved March 29, 2024, from https://infuse.com/insight/the-dos-and-donts-of-channel-marketing/.

"Effective Strategies to Generate Qualified Leads in 2025," *INFUSE*, June 4, 2025. Retrieved August 14, 2025, from https://infuse.com/insight/how-to-generate-qualified-leads/.

"Eliminate Waste and Complexity in Your Digital Advertising Budget," *Proxima*, May 15, 2023. Retrieved March 29, 2024, from https://proximagroup.com/proxima-perspectives/eliminate-waste-and-complexity-in-your-digital-advertising-budget/.

Enge, E. "Mobile vs. Desktop Usage in 2020," *Perficient*, March 23, 2021. Retrieved March 29, 2024, from https://www.perficient.com/insights/research-hub/mobile-vs-desktop-usage.

Fardian, D. "5 Biggest Limitations of Artificial Intelligence," *Glair.ai.*, July 1, 2022. Retrieved March 29, 2024, from https://glair.ai/post/5-biggest-limitations-of-artificial-intelligence.

"Five Intent-Based Marketing Myths: Hype vs Reality," *INFUSE,* August 23, 2021. Retrieved March 28, 2024, from https://infuse.com/insight/five-intent-based-marketing-myths-hype-vs-reality/.

Flynn, J. "28+ Incredible Meeting Statistics [2023]: Virtual, Zoom, In-Person Meetings and Productivity," *Zippia*, July 6, 2023. Retrieved March 29, 2024, from https://www.zippia.com/advice/meeting-statistics/.

Foland, R., Cramer, T., Arnof-Fenn, P., Lim, C., Leibtag, A., Evans, M., Steimle, J., Chopra, V., Bentz, J., Yu, D., Wilson, P., Kim, L., Houlihan, M., McEwen, M., Rubin, T., Zacharaki, V., Beauregard, J., Leonhardt, D., Albert, V., & Trappe, C. "B2B Lead Generation and Demand Generation Strategies for 2022: Recommendations From 20 Industry Experts," *INFUSE*, (n.d.). Retrieved March 28, 2024, from https://infuse.com/insight/b2b-lead-generation-and-demand-generation-strategies-for-2022/.

Freeman, D. 'How to Kickstart Your Demand Generation Strategy for Success: Top of Funnel Guide," *INFUSE*, (n.d.-a). Retrieved March 28, 2024, from https://infuse.com/insight/how-to-kickstart-your-demand-generation-strategy/.

Freeman, D. "RevOps: How to Organize Your Business for Revenue Growth in 2023," *INFUSE*, (n.d.-b). Retrieved January 31, 2025, from https://infuse.com/insight/revops-how-to-organize-your-business-for-revenue-growth/.

Freeman, D., & Sambrook, A. "The Challenges of Demand Generation in 2023: 4 Methods to Drive Growth," *INFUSE*, (n.d.). Retrieved March 28, 2024, from https://infuse.com/insight/demand-generation-challenges/.

"The Great Data Debate—Majority of World Citizens Do Not Trust Their Government," *Lloyd's Register Foundation*, November 25, 2022. Retrieved March 29, 2024, from https://www.lrfoundation.org.uk/en/news/majority-of-world-citizens-do-not-trust-their-governments-with-their-personal-information/.

Gunn, N. "Creating Effective Content for Channel Partners," *Extu*, June 16, 2018. Retrieved February 05, 2025, from https://extu.com/blog/creating-effective-channel-marketing-content/.

Harlow, S. "Summer Slumps: How Can B2B Businesses Deal With Them?" *Sopro*, August 8, 2022. Retrieved March 28, 2024, from https://sopro.io/resources/blog/summer-slumps-how-can-b2b-businesses-deal-with-them/.

Heath, T. "95-5 Rule," *LinkedIn Marketing Solutions*, (n.d.). Retrieved January 27, 2025, from https://business.linkedin.com/marketing-solutions/b2b-institute/b2b-research/trends/95-5-rule.

"Here's the Best Schedule for Lead Follow Up," *Kixie*, (n.d.). Retrieved March 29, 2024, from https://www.kixie.com/sales-blog/heres-the-best-schedule-for-lead-follow-up/.

Holmes, P. "12 Strategies for Return On Ad Spend Optimization," *AdRoll Blog*, January 11, 2023. Retrieved March 29, 2024, from https://www.adroll.com/blog/how-to-optimize-return-on-ad-spend-roas.

"How Long Does It Take to Implement an ERP?" *ERP Research*, September 28, 2022. Retrieved March 29, 2024, from https://www.erpresearch.com/en-us/blog/erp-implementation-time.

"How to Activate Demand Strategies with AI in 2025," *INFUSE*, (s.d.). Retrieved January 31, 2025, from https://infuse.com/insight/how-to-activate-demand-strategies-with-ai/.

"How to Build a B2B Sales Funnel: 5 Templates to Inspire Your High-Converting Marketing Strategy," *INFUSE*, (n.d.). Retrieved March 29, 2024, from https://infuse.com/insight/how-to-build-a-b2b-sales-funnel/.

"How to Create a B2B Sales Funnel: 10 Case Studies," *INFUSE*, (n.d.). Retrieved March 29, 2024, from https://infuse.com/insight/b2b-sales-funnel/.

"How to Develop High-Impact Content for Demand Generation," *INFUSE*, (n.d.). Retrieved March 28, 2024, from https://infuse.com/insight/content-performance/.

"How to Drive CLTV: A Guide to Fostering Brand Evangelism," *INFUSE*, (s.d.). Retrieved January 31, 2025, from https://infuse.com/insight/how-to-drive-cltv/.

"How to Maintain Growth During a Recession: A 3-Step Playbook," *INFUSE*, (n.d.). Retrieved March 29, 2024, from https://infuse.com/insight/how-to-maintain-growth-during-economic-softening-a-3-step-playbook/.

"How to Move Leads Down the Sales Funnel Quickly," *INFUSE*, August 2, 2021. Retrieved March 29, 2024, from https://infuse.com/insight/how -to-move-leads-down-the-sales-funnel-quickly/.

"How to Use Surveys to Gather Actionable Insights," *INFUSE*, (n.d.). Retrieved March 28, 2024, from https://infuse.com/insight/how-to -leverage-surveys/.

"How to Win More Market Share," *INFUSE*, February 12, 2022. Retrieved March 28, 2024, from https://infuse.com/insight/how-to-win-more -market-share/.

"The Importance of Firmographics for B2B Marketing," *INFUSE*, (n.d.). Retrieved March 28, 2024, from https://infuse.com/insight/the -importance-of-firmographics-for-b2b-marketing/.

"*INFUSE* and MOI Global Reflect on the 2023 State of the B2B Market," *INFUSE*, (n.d.). Retrieved March 28, 2024, from https://infuse.com /insight/infuse-and-moi-global-reflect-on-the-2023-state-of-the-b2b -market/.

"*INFUSE* Insights Report: Voice of the Buyer 2025," *INFUSE* (n.d.). Retrieved January 27, 2025, from https://infuse.com/insight/infuse -insights-report-voice-of-the-buyer-2025/.

"*INFUSE* Insights Report: Voice of the Marketer 2025," *INFUSE*, (n.d.). Retrieved January 27, 2025, from https://infuse.com/insight/infuse -insights-report-voice-of-the-marketer-2025/.

Janz, C. "Learning More About That Other Half: The Case for Cohort Analysis and Multi-Touch Attribution Analysis," *Neil Patel* (n.d.). Retrieved March 29, 2024, from https://neilpatel.com/blog /cohort-and-multi-touch-attribution/.

Kesler, A. "10 Top of Funnel Lead Nurturing Best Practices to Boost Your Sales," *INFUSE*, (n.d.-a). Retrieved March 29, 2024, from https: //infuse.com/insight/10-top-of-funnel-lead-nurturing-best-practices-to -boost-your-sales/.

Kesler, A. "Definitive Guide to B2B Account Based Marketing," *INFUSE*. (n.d.-b). Retrieved March 28, 2024, from https://infuse.com/insight /definitive-guide-to-b2b-account-based-marketing/.

Kesler, A. "Definitive Guide to B2B Content Marketing," *INFUSE*, (n.d.-c). Retrieved March 28, 2024, from https://infuse.com/insight/definitive -guide-to-b2b-content-marketing/.

Kesler, A. "Definitive Guide to B2B Lead Generation," *INFUSE,* (n.d.-d). Retrieved March 28, 2024, from https://infuse.com/insight/definitive -guide-to-b2b-lead-generation/.

"Kill the Sales Funnel: Why You Should Rethink this Marketing Method," *INFUSE*, (n.d.). Retrieved March 29, 2024, from https://infuse.com /blog/insight/kill-the-sales-funnel/.

Kim, L. "What's a Good Conversion Rate? (It's Higher Than You Think)," *WordStream*, November 13, 2023. Retrieved March 29, 2024, from https://www.wordstream.com/blog/ws/2014/03/17/what-is-a-good-conversion-rate.

Kumar, D. "Implementing Customer Segmentation Using Machine Learning [Beginners Guide]," *Neptune.ai*, December 19, 2023. Retrieved March 28, 2024, from https://neptune.ai/blog/customer-segmentation-using-machine-learning.

"Lead Generation Tips, Tricks, and Total Domination," *INFUSE*, (n.d.). Retrieved March 29, 2024, from https://infuse.com/insight/lead-generation-tips-tricks-and-total-domination/.

Levin, V. "Is Predictive Intelligence the Future of B2B Marketing?" *HubSpot*, December 6, 2019. Retrieved March 29, 2024, from https://blog.hubspot.com/marketing/is-predictive-intelligence-the-future-of-b2b-marketing.

Litvak, A. "The Ideal Revenue Operations Team Structure for SaaS Companies," *Sightfull*, (n.d.). Retrieved March 29, 2024, from https://www.sightfull.com/blog/revenue-operations-team-structure/.

"Marketing Analytics: What It Is and Why It Matters," *SAS*, (n.d.). Retrieved March 29, 2024, from https://www.sas.com/en_us/insights/marketing/marketing-analytics.html.

"Marketing Data Consolidation: Aggregate, Analyze, and Report in One Place," *tapClicks*, (n.d.). Retrieved March 29, 2024, from https://www.tapclicks.com/resources/blog/marketing-data-consolidation.

"Matillion and IDG Survey: Data Growth Is Real, and 3 Other Key Findings," *Matillion,* January 26, 2022. Retrieved March 29, 2024, from https://www.matillion.com/blog/matillion-and-idg-survey-data-growth-is-real-and-3-other-key-findings.

Meltzer, J. "First-Party Data Offers a Solution for Privacy and Performance," *Think with Google*, December 2020. Retrieved February 03, 2025, from https://www.thinkwithgoogle.com/marketing-strategies/monetization-strategies/first-party-data-transparency/.

Metz, C., Kang, C., Frenkel, S., Thompson, S., & Grant, N. "How Tech Giants Cut Corners to Harvest Data for A.I.," *The New York Times*, April 8, 2024. Retrieved January 31, 2025, from https://www.nytimes.com/2024/04/06/technology/tech-giants-harvest-data-artificial-intelligence.html.

Miller, A. "4 UGC Benefits for B2B Brands," *Walker Sands,* January 28, 2020. Retrieved March 29, 2024, from https://www.walkersands.com/about/blog/4-ugc-benefits-for-b2b-brands/.

"MQAs vs MQLs: How to Identify the Best Leads for ABX," *INFUSE*, (n.d.). Retrieved March 28, 2024, from https://infuse.com/insight/mqas-vs-mqls-how-to-identify-the-best-leads-for-abx/.

"Multi-Touch Attribution: What It Is & How to Use It," *Marketing Evolution*, July 20, 2022. Retrieved March 29, 2024, from https://www.marketingevolution.com/marketing-essentials/multi-touch-attribution.

Murano, R., Roopnarain, B., Yarborough, B., Mortenson, C., Rivera, N., Powers, J., Basu, S., Veerkamp, C., Medley, J., Heyningen, S., Stroup, B., Babu, M., Raleigh, D., III, Manova, K., Hargett, J., Evans, K., Samuel, S., Kelly, M., Stahl, A., ... Yap, A. "B2B Expert Roundup: Top RevOps Trends to Watch in 2023," *INFUSE*, (n.d.). Retrieved March 29, 2024, from https://infuse.com/insight/top-revops-trends-to-watch/.

"Navigating the Attention Economy via Snack-able & Shareable Content," *Demand Gen Report*, 2024. Retrieved January 29, 2025, from https://www.demandgenreport.com/resources/navigating-the-attention-economy-via-snack-able-shareable-content/47367/.

"Navigating the Nature of Nurture," *Twogether.*, (n.d.). Retrieved March 28, 2024, from https://twogether.turtl.co/story/navigating-the-new-nature-of-nurture/page/1.

Needle, F. "What Is Customer Sentiment? [Expert Insight]," *HubSpot*, June 8, 2023. Retrieved March 29, 2024, from https://blog.hubspot.com/service/customer-sentiment.

"New Retail Study Shows Marketers Under-Leverage Emotional Connection," *PR Newswire*, September 27, 2018. Retrieved March 29, 2024, from https://www.prnewswire.com/news-releases/new-retail-study-shows-marketers-under-leverage-emotional-connection-300720049.html.

Nicholson, R. "How to Do A/B Testing: 15 Steps for the Perfect Split Test," *HubSpot*, March 21, 2024. Retrieved March 29, 2024, from https://blog.hubspot.com/marketing/how-to-do-a-b-testing.

Noori, R. "Asana's Celebration Creatures Are More Than Just a Gimmick," *Zapier*, June 9, 2022. Retrieved March 29, 2024, from https://zapier.com/blog/asana-celebrations/.

"Omnichannel Marketing vs Multichannel Marketing: What Is the Difference?" *INFUSE*, (n.d.). Retrieved March 28, 2024, from https://infuse.com/insight/omnichannel-marketing-vs-multichannel/.

"Outlook 2022: What's Next in B2B Marketing?" *INFUSE*, (n.d.). Retrieved March 29, 2024, from https://infuse.com/insight/outlook-2022-whats-next-in-b2b-marketing/.

Paghdal, A. "How To Guest Post (When Everyone Ignores Your Pitches)," *Outreach Labs*, October 5, 2022. Retrieved March 29, 2024, from https://www.outreachlabs.com/guest-posting/how-to-guest-post/.

Parkin, T. "The Marketing Black Box: Why Radical Transparency Is Key," *MarTech,*" February 3, 2022. Retrieved March 29, 2024, from https://martech.org/the-marketing-black-box-why-radical-transparency-is-key/.

"Partner Campaigns: 5 Strategies for Driving Performance," *INFUSE*, (n.d.). Retrieved March 29, 2024, from https://infuse.com/insight/partner-campaigns-5-strategies-for-driving-performance/.

Patterson, C. "Buying Group Marketing: The Next Evolution of ABM," *MarTech*, February 25, 2022. Retrieved March 28, 2024, from https://martech.org/buying-group-marketing-the-next-evolution-of-abm/.

Rajpurohit, M. "The Rise of ABX: How to Achieve True ABM in 2023," *INFUSE,* (n.d.). Retrieved March 28, 2024, from https://infuse.com/insight/the-rise-of-abx-how-to-achieve-true-abm/.

Randolph, K. "Eight Sales and Marketing Vanity Metrics to Avoid at All Costs," *Nutshell*, March 27, 2024. Retrieved March 29, 2024, from https://www.nutshell.com/blog/sales-and-marketing-vanity-metrics.

Reichheld, F. "Prescription for Cutting Costs," *Bain & Company*. (s.d.). Retrieved January 31, 2025, from https://media.bain.com/Images/BB_Prescription_cutting_costs.pdf.

Reijnders, D. "Why You Will Never Again Publish a White Paper as a PDF," *Foleon*, (n.d.). Retrieved March 29, 2024, from https://www.foleon.com/blog/why-you-will-never-again-publish-a-white-paper-as-a-pdf.

Reynolds, K. "Account-Based Marketing and the Inverted Funnel," *OpenMoves,* July 20, 2022. Retrieved March 28, 2024, from https://openmoves.com/blog/account-based-marketing-and-the-inverted-funnel/.

Rioux, P. "The Value of Investing in Loyal Customers," *Forbes,* January 29, 2020. Retrieved January 31, 2025, from https://www.forbes.com/councils/forbesagencycouncil/2020/01/29/the-value-of-investing-in-loyal-customers/.

Sambrook, A. "The Recession: Forging the Right Alliances for Growth in 2023," *INFUSE*, (n.d.). Retrieved March 29, 2024, from https://infuse.com/insight/the-recession-forging-the-right-alliances-for-growth/.

Silva, C., Skopec, C., & Paruch, Z. "What Is Bounce Rate & What Is a Good Rate?" *Semrush (*blog*).* February 29, 2024. Retrieved March 29, 2024, from https://www.semrush.com/blog/bounce-rate/.

"Social Selling: Definitions, Benefits & Tips for Sales Leaders," *LinkedIn Sales Solutions* (s.d.). Retrieved January 31, 2025, from https://business.linkedin.com/sales-solutions/social-selling.

Spencer, E. L. "Sentiment Analysis for Brand Building," *Revuze*, September 9, 2022. Retrieved March 29, 2024, from https://www.revuze.it/blog/sentiment-analysis/.

Stahl, S. "7 Things B2B Content Marketers Need in 2023 [New Research]," *Content Marketing Institute*, October 19, 2022. Retrieved March 29, 2024, from https://contentmarketinginstitute.com/articles/b2b-content-marketing-research-trends-statistics.

Stahl, S. "B2B Content Marketing Benchmarks, Budgets, and Trends: Outlook for 2025," *Content Marketing Institute*, October 9, 2024.

Retrieved January 29, 2025, from https://contentmarketinginstitute. com/articles/b2b-content-marketing-trends-research/.

Stark, S. "5 Keys to Creating Value with First-Party Data," *Think with Google*, March 2021). Retrieved February 03, 2025, from https://www .thinkwithgoogle.com/future-of-marketing/digital-transformation /sustainable-first-party-data-strategy/.

"The State of AI in Demand Generation in 2024: A Practical Approach," *INFUSE,* (s.d.). Retrieved January 31, 2025, from https://infuse.com /insight/the-state-of-ai-in-demand-generation-in-2024/.

"The State of RevOps Report: Reducing Friction In The Flywheel," *HubSpot*, (n.d.). Retrieved March 29, 2024, from https://offers.hubspot .com/rev-ops-report.

Statti, A. "Unlock Your Business Potential with RevOps Consulting," *RevPartners*, (n.d.). Retrieved March 29, 2024, from https://blog .revpartners.io/en/revops-articles/unlock-business-potential-revops -consulting.

Stein, A., Soudak, G., Lev, I., Kranz, J., Boyd, A., Warner, C. D., Anand, S., Chattaway, F., Scarborough, M., Pick, T., Zanotto, G., Apostol, R., Emminizer, J., Shain, H., & Riley, C. "Demand Generation Expert Roundup: Adapting to Challenges in Lead Generation and Demand Marketing in 2022," *INFUSE*, (n.d.). Retrieved March 28, 2024, from https://infuse.com/insight/b2b-expert-roundup/.

Sterling, G. "B2B buyers consume an average of 13 content pieces before deciding on a vendor," *MarTech*, February 14, 2020. Retrieved March 29, 2024, from https://martech.org/b2b-buyers-consume-an-average -of-13-content-pieces-before-deciding-on-a-vendor/.

Thomas, S. "How 4 Brands Consolidated Their Media Buys to Increase Ad Effectiveness and Boost Reach," *Think with Google*, May, 2023. Retrieved March 29, 2024, from https://www.thinkwithgoogle.com /marketing-strategies/data-and-measurement/media-consolidation/.

Timothy, S., Bettencourt, R. M., Straetz, C., Babb, A., French, V., Cojocariu, A., Barudin, M., Ward, C., Wilkinson, V., Goldwater, E., Kernes, K., Palermo, S., & Madden, M. "B2B Expert Roundup: KPI Marketing. Which Demand Marketing KPIs Are Most Impactful for Your Business and Why?" *INFUSE*, (n.d.). Retrieved March 29, 2024, from https://infuse.com/insight/demand-generation-marketing/.

"Top 5 HR Trends and Priorities for 2024," *Gartner*, (n.d.). Retrieved March 29, 2024, from https://www.gartner.com/en/human-resources /trends/top-priorities-for-hr-leaders.

"The Typical Startup Saw a 24% Increase in Sales Cycle in 2023," *Tomasz Tunguz*, March 28, 2023. Retrieved March 29, 2024, from https: //tomtunguz.com/sales_cycle_changes/.

"The Ultimate Guide to Landing Page A/B Testing," *Leadpages,* October 6, 2023. Retrieved March 29, 2024, from https://www.leadpages.com /blog/ab-testing-split-testing.

Vance, J. "Gamification in B2B Marketing: Why You Need It + 8 Real-World Examples," *Jeff Bullas.* March 20, 2024. Retrieved March 29, 2024, from https://www.jeffbullas.com/gamification-in-b2b-marketing/.

Vaughan, P. "30 Thought-Provoking Lead Nurturing Stats You Can't Ignore," *HubSpot*, February 18, 2020. Retrieved March 29, 2024, from https://blog.hubspot.com/blog/tabid/6307/bid/30901/30-thought -provoking-lead-nurturing-stats-you-can-t-ignore.aspx.

Vaughan, R. "How Retargeting Campaigns Help You Reach 98% of Your Site's Visitors," *GoSquared*, (n.d.). Retrieved March 29, 2024, from https://www.gosquared.com/blog/retargeting-visitors.

Verwey, D. "The Readjustment of the Tech Market," *INFUSE* (n.d.). Retrieved March 29, 2024, from https://infuse.com/insight/the -readjustment-of-the-tech-market/.

Verwey, D., Dalton, M., & Gray, S. "The State of Channel in 2023: Challenges and Opportunities," *INFUSE*, (n.d.). Retrieved March 29, 2024, from https://infuse.com/insight/the-state-of-channel-in-2023/.

"What Are Great Channel Marketing Strategies?" *INFUSE*. (n.d.). Retrieved March 29, 2024, from https://infuse.com/insight/what-are -great-channel-marketing-strategies/.

"What Is Demand Generation? Demand Gen vs Lead Gen," *INFUSE*, (n.d.-a). Retrieved March 28, 2024, from https://infuse.com/insight /demand-generation-vs-lead-generation/.

"What Is Demand Generation Marketing? 6-Month B2B Playbook to Drive Brand Awareness at Scale," *INFUSE*, (n.d.). Retrieved March 28, 2024, fromhttps://infuse.com/insight/what-is-demand-generation-marketing/.

"WHM Survey: Half of B2B Decision Makers Bored by B2B Marketing," *WHM Creative*, August 4, 2022. Retrieved March 29, 2024, from https://whmcreative.com/press_release/whm-survey-half-of-b2b -decision-makers-bored-by-b2b-marketing/.

"Why Are Brands Funding Misinformation?" *Forrester*, June 23, 2022. Retrieved March 29, 2024, from https://www.forrester.com/what-it -means/ep273-marketing-funding-misinformation/.

"Why the Relationship Funnel Matters: A 4-Step Playbook for Generating Multiple Leads per Account," *INFUSE*. (n.d.). Retrieved January 31, 2025, from https://infuse.com/insight/relationship-funnel/.

Zaiceva, A. "How to Build an Omnichannel Marketing Strategy," *INFUSE*, (n.d.). Retrieved March 28, 2024, from https://infuse.com /insight/how-to-build-an-omnichannel-marketing-strategy/.

ACRONYM GLOSSARY

ABM	Account-Based Marketing
ABX	Account-Based Experience
ACV	Annual Contract Value
AEO	Answer Engine Optimization
AI	Artificial Intelligence
AIDA	Attention, Interest, Desire, and Action
AIO	Activities, Interests, and Opinions
B2B	Business-to-Business
B2C	Business-to-Consumer
BOFU	Bottom of Funnel
CAC	Client Acquisition Costs
CCPA	California Consumer Privacy Act
CFO	Chief Financial Officer
CLTV	Client Lifetime value
CMO	Chief Marketing Officer
COO	Chief Operating Officer
CPL	Cost Per Lead
CRM	Client Relationship Management
CSR	Corporate Social Responsibility
CTA	Call To Action
CX	Client Experience
DevOps	Developer Operations
ERP	Enterprise Resource Planning
ESG	Environmental, Social, and Governance
FAQ	Frequently Asked Questions
FinOps	Financial Operations
GDPR	General Data Protecion Regulation
GEO	Generative Engine Optimization
GPT	Generative Pre-trained Transformer
H2H	Human-to-Human

HR	Human Resources
ICP	Ideal Client Profile
IT	Information Technology
KPI	Key Performance Indicator
M&A	Mergers and Acquisitions
MDF	Marketing Development Funds
ML	Machine Learning
MOFU	Middle of Funnel
MQA	Marketing Qualified Account
MQL	Marketing Qualified Lead
NLP	Natural Language Processing
PPC	Pay-Per-Click
Q&A	Questions and Answers
RACE	Reach, Act, Convert, and Engage
RevOps	Revenue Operations
ROAS	Return on Ad Spend
ROI	Return on Investment
ROR	Return on Relationship
SaaS	Software as a Service
SAR	Subject Access Request
SDR	Sales Development Representative
SEM	Search Engine Marketing
SEO	Search Engine Optimization
SERP	Search Engine Results Page
SLA	Service Level Agreement
SQL	Sales Qualified Lead
SSoT	Single Source of Truth
STEM	Science, Technology, Engineering, and Mathematics
SWOT	Strengths, Weaknesses, Opportunities, and Threats
TAM	Total Addressable Market
TOFU	Top of Funnel
UGC	User-Generated Content
UVP	Unique Value Proposition
UX	User Experience

INDEX

social media in, 42–43
unique value proposition in, 33
user experiences in, 35–36
demand intelligence, 105–106
dynamic content, 67

E

earned content distribution, 42
eBooks, 63
economic uncertainty, 155
educational content, 64–65
email, in demand generation, 42–43
email personalization, 105
emotion detection, 145
employee resilience, to change, 162–163
events, 74–75

F

feature creep, 49
feedback, content adjustment from, 64
fine-grained analysis, 145
firmographic segmentation, 11–12
first-touch attribution, 39
follow-up, in relationship building, 110–111
Forrester model, 91
freezing, of marketing campaigns, 155
full-path attribution, 39

G

gamification, 110
generative AI, 61–62
geographic segmentation, 12

H

heavy users, 15
high-value accounts, 47
how-to guides, 65
HubSpot flywheel, 93

human-to-human marketing, 104–105

I

ICPs. *See* ideal client profiles (ICPs)
ideal client profiles (ICPs)
attributes in, 7–8
audience's preferred communication channels and, 6
ideal, 3–10
pain points in, 8
personas and, 3–4
surveys with, 6–7
influencer partnerships, 69, 77
influencers, of purchase behavior, 14
intent, as asset, 52
intent, tracking online behavior to understand, 15–16
invisible buyers, 88–90

K

key performance indicators (KPIs)
in channel and partner marketing, 81
competitor, 141–142
data sources in, 134
in demand generation, 43, 132
most beneficial, 131–133
relationship building and, 103
in revenue operations, 123–124
strategy-cost correlations and, 135–136
vanity metrics *vs.*, 133
knowledge bases, 65

L

landing pages, 146
last-touch attribution, 39
lead capture page, 37
lead scoring, 17–18
linear attribution, 39
long-form content, 62–63

M

marketing qualified accounts (MQAs), 50, 144
marketing qualified leads (MQLs), 21, 86–88, 96, 126, 144
McKinsey model, 91
middle of the sales funnel (MOFU), 30–31, 37, 57, 94
misinformation, 163–164
mobile users, responsive design for, 59
MOFU. *See* middle of the sales funnel (MOFU)
MQAs. *See* marketing qualified accounts (MQAs)
MQLs. *See* marketing qualified leads (MQLs)
multi-touch attribution, 140

N

natural language processing (NLP), 20, 41, 107
negative buyer personas, 5
neuromarketing, 160–161
niche marketing, 18–19
NLP. *See* natural language processing (NLP)
North Star, 29–30

O

occasional users, 15
omnichannel marketing, 96
onboarding, 137, 149–150
online behavior, tracking of, 15–16
owned content distribution, 42

P

paid advertising, 36–37
paid content distribution, 43
pain points, client, 8
pay-per-click (PPC), 36, 136
performance measurement, 70–71
personalized content, 67

personas
  by audience segment, 9
  buyer, 4–5
  negative, 5
  revenue operations and, 122
  role of, client profiles and, 3–4
  types of, 5
  updating, 9–10
pillar pages, 62–63
PPC. *See* pay-per-click (PPC)
predictive analytics, 143–144
pricing, client demographics and, 147
privacy, data, 152–153
privacy regulations, 23–24
product positioning, 18–19
prospects, by geographic segmentation, 12
psychographics, 14

Q

qualification models, buyer-centric, 21

R

RACE MODEL, 92
referral marketing, 69, 79–80
referral programs, 137
regular users, 15
regulation, of AI, 158–159
relationship building
  action in, 103
  attention and, 103
  automation software and, 114–115
  chatbots in, 107
  client lifetime value and, 100
  consistent communication in, 115–116
  conversations in, 111–112
  demand intelligence and, 105–106
  desire in, 103
  email personalization in, 105
  follow-up in, 110–111

gamification in, 110
human-to-human marketing
    and, 104–105
interest in, 103
nurturing in, 106–107, 113–114
obstacles in, 112–113
retargeting in, 109
sales cycles and, 114–115
social media in, 106
social networks in, 108
strategy, 103–104
touchpoints in, 108–109
trust in, 111–112
resilience, to change, 162–163
resource centers, 65
retargeting, 109
return on investment (ROI), 22, 25,
    27, 36, 43, 72, 86, 123–124
return on relationship (ROR),
    103–104
revenue growth, 124
revenue operations (RevOps)
    buyer personas and, 122
    client experience and, 118–119
    content marketing and, 125
    defined, 117
    experts in, 127–128
    process definition in, 120–121
    responsibility definition in,
        120–121
    role definition in, 120–121
    silos and, 120
    team structure, 121
    user experience and, 119
revenue retention, 124
ROI. *See* return on investment
    (ROI)
ROR. *See* return on relationship
    (ROR)

S
sales development representatives
    (SDRs), 46

sales-led journeys, 86
sales qualified leads (SQLs), 86–87,
    96, 126
sales teams, in content creation,
    66–67
scoring, lead, 17–18
SDRs. *See* sales development
    representatives (SDRs)
semiotics, 160–161
sentiment analysis, 144–145
silos, 120
social listening, 4, 41–42, 89–90
social media
    in account-based marketing,
        46–47
    in demand generation, 42–43
    in relationship building, 106
social proofing, 18
social sharing, 89–90
stakeholders, in account-based.
    marketing, 46
style guide, for content, 56–57
style guidelines, in marketing
    communications, 34–35
surveys, 4–7

T
TAM. *See* total addressable market
    (TAM)
targeting
    account scoring in, 17–18
    by account status, 14–15
    artificial intelligence in, 19–20
    audience demographics in, 13
    behavioral patterns in, 16–17
    buyer-centric qualification
        models in, 21
    buyer intent and, 15–16
    data cleansing in, 20–21
    data leveraging in, 11–25
    data segmentation in, 19–20
    influencers in, 14
    lead scoring in, 17–18

NOTES

NOTES

NOTES

NOTES

NOTES

NOTES

NOTES

NOTES

NOTES

NOTES

NOTES

NOTES

NOTES

NOTES

NOTES

NOTES

NOTES

NOTES

NOTES